SAFE LANDING

*A family's journey following the crash
of American Airlines Flight 191*

Thanks for being part,
of our journey!
♡
Melody Smith
Jim Borchers
Kim Jnkl

2011

Printed in the United States of America
First Edition
ISBN 978-1-7365769-3-9

Cover design and typesetting by Annie Leue
longoverduebooks.com

This book is dedicated to Mom and Dad and the 271 other individuals who died with them on May 25, 1979 and to all those who crossed our paths and helped us in some way, along our Flight 191 journey. "We don't meet people by accident. They are meant to cross our path for a reason." It's a Wonderful Life.

We would like to acknowledge our spouses: Bob, Jennifer, & Pete and our families for encouraging us to tell our story. The photo on the cover is the last photo taken of our parents at a wedding a week prior to the crash. We hope they are still dancing.

MELODY, JIM, & KIM

TABLE OF CONTENTS

The Crash 7

Searching for Mom and Dad 29

We All Need to be Strong 37

Farewell to Our Childhood Home 45

Showing Up 55

Going There: Our Journey Back to the Crash 65

Finish the Flight 83

Permanent Marker 91

Sixth Grade Heroes 101

The Stars Align 113

Miracles Do Happen 123

A Place to Gather 133

The Grand Reveal 147

APPENDIX 159

ACKNOWLEDGMENTS 175

The CRASH

KIM ◆ As the stewardess made final take-off announcements, I looked to my right and left. Every time I've flown since that fateful day, I have the same ritual; I count the seconds as the plane increases speed down the runway.

29.

30.

31.

Thirty-one seconds. This was the amount of time the DC-10 airplane was in the air before losing its left engine and crashing in a field north of the runway at O'Hare airport. The crash's impact was so intense there was little left of those on the flight, and debris was scattered everywhere. All 271 passengers and crew on board — and two individuals on the ground — lost their lives.

A DC-10 was broken apart, lives were lost, and all the lives of families and friends would be forever altered after the crash of American Airlines Flight 191. It is still the worst non-terrorist-related crash in American history.

Yet there we were, 25 years later, clicking our seat belts on an American Airlines flight. My sister and I, along with our families, were off to witness our brother Jim's wedding in Hawaii, the same destination our parents (known as "Nudy" and Bill) left for on May 25th, 1979.

JIM ♦ In September of 1978, I was 29-years-old, single, and managing one of the most popular late-night bars in all of Chicago. I shared a very large apartment with a college friend on the "Near North" side, just steps away from Lincoln Park and Lake Michigan. In Chicago, proximity to the lake is everything.

I'd become a serious runner competing almost every weekend in 10k races around the city. I'd been training for several years to compete in the new Mayor Daley Marathon (later called the Chicago Marathon). I finished my first marathon with a respectable time of 3 hours, 29 minutes. Not bad for my first time!

But the highlight of the day occurred at the 18-mile mark. This is a critical point in a marathon when many runners "hit the wall." As I approached the 18-mile marker, Mom and Dad were there to cheer me on. They were easy to spot in the sizable crowd because "Nudy" was doing a headstand! Needless to say, I picked up the pace, and I'm sure I had a big grin on my face for the next several miles.

Headstand in a crowd of people? That was just a typically eccentric and supportive act we were all accustomed to as the children of Nudy and Bill.

MELODY ♦ One of my fondest memories of Mom standing on her head was in 8th grade. Our family was celebrating St. Patrick's Day at a local restaurant in our parish called Deasy's. The owner was a rather stern Irishman but was fond of Nudy, as all the adults called her. Mom gave me a "head's up" that the owner had asked her to stand on her head as part of the St. Patrick's Day festivities. Mom told me she'd be wearing a taffeta green dress and was going to let her skirt fall to display a ruffled green undergarment with a shamrock on her backside. She wanted me to be prepared when her skirt fell in front of a couple hundred parishioners.

Don't worry, it's all planned.

Needless to say, as a teenager with some of my classmates present, I was *slightly* embarrassed. But I was proud of how Mom could do something this crazy with style and grace.

KIM ◆ Or how about this one time after a Cubs game; if my memory serves me right, the game went into extra innings, and, back then, there was no cut-off for beers served at Wrigley Field. The raucous crowd was in full party mode.

After the game, we all went across the street to the Sports Corner at Sheffield and Addison for additional cheers and fun. We were all singing and dancing and then, next thing you know Melody, Mom, and I were standing on our heads on top of the bar! The place went wild!

MELODY ◆ No other moms I knew during the '50s were focusing on yoga. Mom taught us the lotus position and the infamous headstand. We would be at picnics with other families, she would clap her hands, and then, like a performing circus, we would all go stand on our heads. All the other kids and adults would try this out, and then Mom would help them learn the proper technique.

Mom and Dad were both very personable and easy to know to the outside world. Dad was genuinely easy-going. He was always there to help, whether taking kids waiting at bus stops to school or helping at our parish with various requests. He would also help neighbors and friends with any breakdowns in their homes. When I was a youngster, I truly felt there wasn't anything Dad couldn't fix or do.

Mom had a much stronger personality, yet she was very likable and fun. The only exception was when things weren't done to her specifications. That's when her Irish temper would come out. I grew up knowing Mom was not afraid to stand up for you if it was deserved. She always had your back.

And perhaps the most memorable (and most mysterious) example of Mom having my back was in January of 1979 — four months before the crash — when Mom wrote me a letter commemorating my 32nd birthday. This letter would ultimately guide my life for decades to come.

Mom often wrote notes on cards, but this was a 2-page typed letter. I can't remember her ever writing something like this before. In this letter, she shared many thoughts. She gave me directions on taking care of our family when she was no longer around or able. She stressed the importance of having patience and always making the effort to get the family together.

I knew Mom had a few reservations about this second honeymoon trip, but this was the first time she talked about her mortality, at least to me. I remember reading her letter and thinking I wouldn't have to worry about these things for many, many years.

Little did I know, this letter would be read at their memorial service, and become my personal directive only four months later:

> *I guess that's what I'm trying to say in this note, I will keep on getting us together as long as God gives me the strength. After I can no longer do this, or yes after I'm gone, I would like you to take the torch, my firstborn, and keep on trying to get them together, not only for the fun of it, but also for the love of it. Maybe one day not so far in the future, both Kim and Jim will be married and you will have a whole gang to round up.*

> *Please remember my request and try to comply. It will take patience on your part, but I know you can do it Mel. I don't have too much to leave the three of you except my love for all of you and my pride in all of you and I hope that carries over to your children and their children.*

> *Your Loving Mom,*
> *Grandma Nudy*

JIM • Mom and Dad's house at 5508 N. California Avenue is a significant part of our story. It was the one and only home we all had known.

Mom and Dad built their home on the GI Bill in 1946, as Dad had served on an LST in World War II. That house became such a touchstone or home base for all of us. In my mind, it would always be there, always be "home." No matter what else was going on in our lives, good or bad, we could always go home.

As Mel and I were now out of the house, and Kim would soon be once she graduated college, the gatherings at 5508 N. California became

January 1979

Reflections on my life as a mother
or a few thoughts from the Irma Brombeck
of Budlong. These flash backs coming to
the fore after celebrating Melody's 32nd
birthday.

Dear Melody:

I now realize that I know you more than half of my life. It certainly would
be hard for you to know the Nudy that lived before she met Bill and before
she would be blessed with a most beautiful little girl and we would call her
Melody. Nudy Ryan was quite a "swinger" or maybe a flapper in her twenties.
The important things to her were her job - car - clothes - mink coat - trips
and fun at bars and places very much like today's single bars. This was her
lifestyle. My only experience with babies up to this point was being around
when Pat was born. But like everyone, I wasn't much interested and didn't
offer to do too much baby sitting and besides at that time I was attending
Northwestern. Rah! Rah!

So when dear Melody came along my entire life changed - I had to give up my
job withthe City at 7 1/2 months pregnant because it was not considered good
taste to work closer to the delivery date. My husband was only eleven months
old, our house was in the process of being built and besides that new husband
was a travelling salesman. Talk about being nervous and anxious - no wonder
you were colic - you sensed all those anxieties in your Mama. This was indeed a lot different than baby Pat - this was my baby and now I found that
there was a purpose to my life and I wanted more than anything to be an especially good Mother. Unfortunately there is no place to go to learn parent-
ing. I guess it's something you pick up as you go along. You learn and
grow with that baby each day as it learns and grows. How lucky for us that
baby Melody grew so beautifully, I did it at thirty one and you will too.
Caring for Jim as a baby seemed like a breeze because now I was a "pro" or
at least I thought I was. Kim's arrival found me a little rusty at the
skills and yes, somewhat nervous again because she was such a wee one.

At the birth of each of you Gram went bananas - my how she loved you all.
She once told me that she really never cared that much about children - my
Dad on the other hand would have loved having a bunch. The feeling for grandchildren however was entirely different she said, and at the time I thought it
strange. To be one is to know one and understand. Even though I love the
three of you equally and dearly , little Christopher has a special love all
his own and he has his own niche in my heart. I'm sure your Dad feels this
too.

We did so enjoy having you all but especially Chris (we hadn't seen him since
Xmas Eve because of the snow) and this year is different because we don't see
him once a week. We wouldn't have cared had he awakened at 3:00 A.M. because
we love him so and we think he likes us. Just wish I could squeeze him more.

12

Hope you enjoyed your entry into your 33rd year, as Gram would say. Sorry the dinner was a little delayed because of our dear Jim. It upsets Dad especially and me a little too, but when he does arrive, I am so glad to see him everything is A-Ok. I do keep on encouraging him to come for all the "red letter" days because we are family and I love when we are all together. Jim just doesn't have too much in common with any of us at the moment - that too will change one day. Now his lifestyle is a complete reversal from any of ours but we all know that he does love us very much. You will remember this one day Mel when Chris is maybe twenty-nine and he breezes in - you won't care that he might be late, only that he's there. You love them when they're little and love them even more when they are big.

I guess that's what I'm trying to say in this note. I will keep on getting us together as long as God gives me the strength. After I can no longer do this or yes , even after I am gone, I would like you to take the torch, my first born and keep on trying to get them together, not only for the fun of it, but also for the love of it. Maybe one day not so far into the future, both Kim and Jim will be married and you will have a whole gang to round up.

Plese remember my request and do try to comply. It will take patience on your part, but I know you can do it Mel. I don't have too much to leave the three of you except my love for all of you and my pride in all of you and I hope that carries over to your children and their children.

Your loving Mom,

Grandma Nudy

Grandma Nudy.

Letter to Melody

from mom

more and more important. We grew up with every holiday, birthday, graduation, and what my parents called "Red Letter Days" celebrated there. That
house was an absolute, a given that you could always count on.

MELODY ◆ Mom coined the term "Red Letter Day." These were positive and meaningful days in our lives — birthdays, holidays, dance recitals,
sports championships, good grades — these were all "Red Letter Days!"

I remember preparations for my birthday parties were almost as
fun as the actual day. Mom included me when deciding the party's theme
along with making the decorations, party favors, and games or activities.
With my birthday being in January, there were a lot of winter themes —
snowmen, ice skating, etc.

It was rare for a month to go by without some type of party in
our house.

KIM ◆ I was the youngest of us three, still living at home with Mom
and Dad. That year, 1979, was shaping up to be a big year in my life. I was
completing my bachelor's degree to become a teacher and was to be married on June 2nd.

Mother's Day, 1979 (left)

Sometime around late summer, early fall of 1978, I decided to call off the wedding. The decision, as I recall, was mutual. We gave our best shot at a long-distance romance, but, in my heart, I knew that as crazy as we were about each other at the onset of our meeting, I didn't want to move to Boston, and my then-fiancé, Michael, was not thrilled about a move to Chicago. Plus, I was excited about starting my student teaching and graduating. We canceled the banquet hall, but not the church.

At first, Mom was very disappointed. She was crazy about my Irish fiancé. And, for someone who had as much fun as she did planning birthday parties, imagine what she could do with a wedding! When Mom eventually came to terms with the cancellation (harder for her than for me!), she insisted we should all go on a trip. But as we looked at calendars, Mom and Dad decided to take an overdue second honeymoon trip to Hawaii, and I booked a trip to Mexico with my friends.

I ended up on a very early flight to Acapulco, Mexico with two girlfriends, Colleen and Kathy. This was May 23rd, two days before my parents boarded American Airlines Flight 191. Ironically, I was staying at a beach resort owned by American Airlines.

Our first day of arrival was unpacking, getting the lay of the land,

and heading out for dinner and drinks. While enjoying the Acapulco nightlife, we ran into John, a friend of my brother's who was vacationing as well, staying one resort over from ours. I'm pretty sure we all stayed up until sunrise.

But, even though we were 23-years-old and full of all that youthful energy, we still decided to catch up on sleep poolside, soaking in as much of the Mexican sun as possible.

On May 25th, I felt a strange sensation come over me out of no-where. It's difficult to explain how I felt as a wave of nausea and faintness riveted through my body. I remember telling Colleen I thought I better go back to our room to lay down. Probably too much sun, Mexican water, and fun the night before. She decided to return for a nap as well, resting up for our evening plans. We both laid down and fell asleep. I'm not sure how long we'd been napping when our hotel phone rang.

MELODY ◆ It was a clear and sunny yet cool day for the beginning of a Memorial Day weekend. This year would be different since Mom and Dad, who always had the first picnic of the summer on Memorial Day weekend, were breaking from tradition with their trip to Hawaii. This was just the third vacation they'd taken, as a couple, in 33 years of marriage.

Mom called at 9:00 AM to say goodbye, and I was heading out the door for my morning jog. We talked general "happy talk" about enjoying themselves on this trip and how Dad was up at the crack of dawn, as he always was. The taxi would be picking them up at 10:30 AM.

Mom said she couldn't believe they were finally going. For months, the trip had been in a constant state of flux of going or not going. Mom still had reservations about it all. She felt guilty leaving us all on a major holiday. I kept reassuring her it was fine. I was 32. Jim was 29. Kim was 23. It was okay. But Mom would forever have excuses and was a bit of a worrier.

She even told me where she hid her jewelry in the basement! Hidden under a part of the ceiling. She talked about her funeral arrangements. I understand this type of thinking far better now in my 70s than I did at 32. At the time, I remember thinking it was ridiculous. I was a little annoyed, too, though I know Mom didn't know it. But, in fairness, Mom had just lost a dear friend, and it upset her terribly. She was upset about the open casket and told me, during this last phone call, to only have the casket open at her wake "if she looked good." Otherwise, "you must have it closed, Mel."

My son, Christopher, who was almost two and was just starting to talk, got on the phone as he started doing the last few months. That last call was the first time he said, "Hi, Grandma Nudy!" Mom was thrilled and said she couldn't wait to get back and see him. She said by then he would be talking in full sentences. My husband, Bob, had taken the day off and was making signals to me to say goodbye so we could proceed with the things we were going to do that morning. He often did this as Mom and I talked to each other just about every day and could talk about everything and nothing for hours. I dismissed him and proceeded to talk to Dad, who said goodbye and shared how they were really excited about this trip (he didn't have the same level of worries as Mom). I said goodbye, they said they'd call Jim next, and that we would see them in 10 days.

JIM ◆ My phone rang early the morning of May 25th. Dad told me I didn't have to take them to the airport. They knew I'd worked late the night before, and they were headed out early via cab.

"Are you sure?" I asked.

"Yes!" Dad confirmed.

I told him to have a great trip, and I'd see them when they got back. I didn't talk to Mom.

Later that day, I walked into the bar I managed to prepare banks and schedules for the night. I passed one television in the back of the bar as I headed upstairs. The image on the TV was of smoke in a field with the caption underneath: "Plane Crash at O'Hare."

At first, it didn't really register. But as I sat there counting out money for the night registers, the TV image started to gnaw at me. I knew Mom and Dad were at the airport early, but I wasn't sure of their flight time. To arrest my fears, I called Melody.

I couldn't get hold of Melody and, back in 1979, there were no answering machines or cell phones. The only person I could think to call was Melody's mother-in-law, Marge. Marge didn't even know our parents were leaving, but she told me she'd try to get hold of Mel and Bob.

Melody called me shortly after, informing me that Mom and Dad's flight was scheduled for around 3 PM, but she was unsure of the airline. She was going to check with the travel agent and call me back.

MELODY ◆ I got off the phone and told Bob my fear that Mom and Dad were on that plane. I called American Airlines and said I wanted information on the crash. They just took my name and number. In the meantime, a very good friend of Mom and Dad's called. She said she'd been trying to get a hold of us all day. She was frantic and felt, for sure, they were on that flight. I assured her I didn't think so but had to get off the line because the airlines would be calling me back.

I remember sitting on our stairway in the hall and saying over and over, "I know they are on that flight. I know they are on that flight," and just waiting. I called American again, and it was the same thing. They said they'd get back to me as soon as possible. I called my mom's sister, Patty.

She'd been out to dinner with Mom and Dad the night before. Maybe she would put my fears to rest. She didn't think it could be true. Didn't think they were on that flight.

I remember catching snatches of scenes of the crash on our television set. I was watching but not concentrating.

Then the travel agent called back and said, "Your mom and dad were scheduled for the flight. American Airlines Flight 191."

I remember yelling, "Oh no! Are you sure?"

Bob took the phone to hear it for himself. I immediately called Jim. There was a lot of background noise at Jim's bar, but I was able to communicate my thoughts, ones I was working through as I spoke.

Here's what I knew:

The crash was American Airlines Flight 191.

This was the flight Mom and Dad were scheduled to be on.

There was still a *chance* they'd missed it, but because they'd left their house so early, that didn't seem likely.

And, if they had missed it by some quirk, they would have called us to tell us they were safe by now.

"You've got to be sure, Melody," Jim said. "Don't say this unless you are sure!"

I will never forget the agony in my brother's voice.

"It cannot be!" he shouted. "I'm going out to the airport to find them, hold them, and comfort them."

"Okay, please don't forget about me. Call me and let me know what's going on at the airport. I'll stay home and wait for the phone call from the airline, actually confirming their deaths. Until then, we won't give up hope."

We both agreed we wouldn't call Kim until it was officially confirmed. There was still the possibility that their travel agent had it wrong...

Bob called our friends who we were scheduled to have dinner with later that evening. Coincidentally, our friend was an attorney for another airline. He said he would try and help us in any way since he was familiar with airline crashes and all the procedures and problems involved. Bob called his folks. They said they would come right over. I called my mom's sister, Patty, and one of our best friends in the area to stay with our son, Christopher. And that was it. I wanted to keep our telephone line open.

Our friends knew and loved my folks. Mom and Dad were the kind of people who easily bridged all age differences. Sure, they were my parents, but they had become my dear friends with whom I could completely be myself. I felt so fortunate that I'd reached that point in a child/parent relationship. As an adult, partying with Mom and Dad was very natural, and they always wanted me and Bob's friends to come to their picnics, parties, and events.

I remember all those Sundays in late summer and early fall, Bob and I, plus two of our favorite couples, would meet Dad at the tennis courts and play round-robin games for hours. We'd go back to Mom and Dad's house, where Mom had prepared a delicious lunch. We'd play backyard games like croquet or volleyball.

And, of course, St. Patrick's Day. That was always a big deal before we had kids. We'd meet Mom and Dad at Johnny Lattner's on the Chicago River with our friends for brunch, and then Dad would lead us to where they were staging the parade. We'd join in carrying our big Shamrock Irish Flag. This was when St. Patrick's Day was celebrated on the actual day, and things were very loose on who was allowed to march in the parade.

Our friends loved Mom and Dad, so it was no surprise how supportive they were in those chaotic hours trying to gather information. I started getting more phone calls from Mom and Dad's friends. Our friends, the Murphys, came right over. I wanted to keep things short and not say too much until we knew with 100 percent certainty that they were physically on Flight 191.

Bob's parents arrived. I know Christopher must have been there, but I was really only aware of my own presence. I'm sure I was trying to make everyone feel comfortable, but I was getting myself under control internally. Deep down, I knew there would be many decisions to make.

But first things first. My brother called at about 8:00 PM. He was at the airport and said he'd been ushered into a VIP room. He was given no information other than a gruesome reminder that bodies were still being gathered. Jim said they were making a list of the passengers by comparing their actual list at check-in to their computer list.

As I talked to Jim, he said their names had just come up on the computer.

C. Borchers and W. Borchers were passengers on American Airlines Flight 191.

There it was. Final confirmation. What I knew at a gut level was now officially true.

"Bob and I will meet you at the airport," I told Jim. Then I called Kim in Mexico.

"Kim, I have some bad news," I said.

I gathered my breath, steadied my voice, and continued with the terrible news.

KIM ◆ When I answered the phone, I thought it was probably John calling about getting together later. Instead, half asleep, I could hear my sister's voice.

Am I still asleep? Why is she calling me?

"There has been a terrible accident, and Mom and Dad are dead," Melody said. "They were killed in a plane crash."

I had difficulty processing what she was saying, but the same wave of faintness and nausea I experienced by the pool earlier (which was right around the time of the crash) poured through my body. I couldn't feel anything except my heart pounding.

Plane crash.

Mom and Dad.

On the flight.

No survivors.

There are snippets of that night, most of it a blur. My body went into shock, and I was trembling, crying. Colleen found John at the resort next door, and he helped find a doctor to give me a sedative. Then my brother called, and I remember just saying, "No, it can't be true!"

After his call, I remember looking out at a religious statue right outside our balcony. In my mind, I was trying to talk to Mom and Dad through the statue.

I don't remember packing a bag or preparing to go back. I do remember the hotel initially saying there was no crash that they knew of, even though they were an American Airlines hotel.

The hotel made arrangements to get me back to Chicago.

MELODY ◆ Bob and I left for the airport.

When I walked into the terminal, I wanted everyone to know what had happened. For me, the whole world had stopped. The fact that it was business as usual for everyone else was unfathomable to me.

I met my brother in the VIP room. Some people represented themselves as American Airlines. They took down information about who I was and gave me a card. They told us, at this time, no bodies would be released.

We still had no idea the magnitude of the crash. We still believed they were just getting all the people together, not realizing they had no identifiable people at this point. Some of Jim's friends were there, and I remember a minister/priest coming to give us comfort. I was only half-listening to what he said, trying to be polite, yet feeling he didn't say a damn thing to me that helped. I wish I could remember the other people in this VIP room. Normally, I always remember faces, but I can't remember seeing anyone else there. We finally told Jim we were heading home to get some sleep and would be in touch tomorrow. Hopefully, Kim would be home, and we could claim Mom and Dad's bodies.

My oldest and dearest girlfriend, Mary, was there when we arrived home. She always was like a member of our family. When she heard the news, she drove for miles to our house, getting lost in the process. After a bit of conversation, everyone went home.

I never ate or slept that night. Bob and I lay there talking about Mom and Dad. I told Bob how I had the worry of Mom and Dad dying on my mind recently. It was a thought that came up several times while working at the office. And now here I was telling everyone that Mom and Dad were dead. Those worries and this disaster felt like they were in some way connected. I told myself, "You must really be trying hard to feel sorry for yourself." A million thoughts go through our minds every day. If Mom and Dad hadn't died, I wouldn't be reflecting back on this at all.

But I still wonder if, somehow, at a subconscious level, I was preparing myself for their deaths.

I got up early in the morning and called a friend of mine who was a Chicago cop. She knew and loved Mom and Dad. She gave me some tips on the procedures of identifying the bodies and where they would typically go. She knew people who had been at the crash site and softly noted, "Melody, I hate to tell you this, but there was not much there that looked like human beings." She gave me the man's name to contact at the coroner's office. She told me to gather whatever information we could for Mom and Dad - medical, dental, etc. She would be in touch and would find out whatever she possibly could. I have to say, she was probably the most helpful in making me realize all that lay ahead and all the data we would need.

I called Jim and gave him the man's name at the coroner's office. He called him and was told to get dental charts. Jim said he would take care of that today. We would only have records for Mom, as Dad had false teeth prior to going overseas during World War II. But it was a start. Our friend, the attorney with another airline, called and said he would try to find out whatever he could. I can remember being upset with him, though he didn't know it, after he told me, "Melody, you are not going to get your folks today, tomorrow, or next week. It's going to be weeks before they can identify 270 some people." I remember thinking, "You don't know what the hell you're talking about!" But oh, how right he was.

I think, maybe with that phone call, I started to understand that the burial of Mom and Dad would not be handled in any standard way.

I called the funeral directors who knew Mom's family for years as well as Dad's. They were shocked and said they'd find out whatever they could and they'd be available to us in whatever capacity needed. Jim called and said he would bring Mom's dental charts to the airport when we went to pick up Kim. He was also going to pick up my Aunt Pat and bring her to our house. My in-laws came to take care of Christopher as the phone calls kept coming. Friends of my folks were all crying in disbelief. They all wanted to know what we were doing. I kept saying, "After today, we'll have a better idea." Plus, Kim was coming in today, and she should be part of that decision.

Then I received a phone call from a woman who said we'd spoken last night in the VIP room. She needed some information about Mom and Dad. She started asking about who their children were, their ages, etc. When she asked me how much money Dad earned, I questioned her. She told me she wasn't with the airlines but rather with the insurance company. I told her I had nothing more to say to her. She had no information on the identification of Mom and Dad, and when I asked her where dental charts and medical records should be delivered, she gave me an address in New York! That was the beginning of my bad feelings toward both the insurance company and American Airlines. I don't know, somehow finding my parents seemed a lot more important to me than how much money they earned. It hadn't even been 24 hours since the crash! You would think they could give us a little more time to process.

KIM ♦ As I said before, I have no recollection of packing or getting to the airport. I remember hugging John, Kathy, and Colleen, saying goodbye, and boarding the plane myself.

I was immediately put in first-class and drank a lot of rum and Diet Cokes. A stewardess sat with me most of the flight. She knew two of the flight crew on Flight 191. I never got her name, but I remember her more than once telling me that the crash happened so fast she was sure they didn't suffer or know what happened.

The entire flight home, I kept reliving all of Mom's concerns about taking the trip. She felt their flight had changed too many times, and this was a constant worry of hers, and I kept assuring her everything would be okay, and they should go. She always had a bad feeling about going.

I still couldn't wrap my head around what had happened. I hadn't seen any news coverage or papers describing the accident. Melody, Jim, and Bob (my brother-in-law) met me at the terminal gate. I remember having this last bit of hope, thinking maybe they'd greet me with news that Mom and Dad were hurt but not dead. Or perhaps they were not on the flight after all. Maybe they had it all wrong...

Unfortunately, the news only got darker. Not only were my parents dead, but there were no bodies. Jim brought Mom's dental records. Police and fire combed the crash site attempting to find body parts to ID 273 people.

MELODY ◆ The representative ushered us into a small conference room to get more information about Mom and Dad. Height, weight, any operations, scars, any jewelry they would have been wearing, etc. Mom had more of a medical history than Dad, who had always been healthy. Plus, as mentioned earlier, Dad had no dental records.

This meeting was a real shock for my sister, as she had no idea how bad the crash had been, even on the plane coming home. I remember Jim being concerned about leaving the dental charts with this man, as it was not the name of the fellow he had been given. He did it anyway, and the man said these were the first dental charts they had received.

This was 4:00 PM Saturday. The crash was at 3:04 PM on Friday. We still had not received an official call from the airlines, and, to this day, we never have.

Kim stayed with us. She couldn't stop shaking, and she was sick to her stomach for days and was afraid to sleep alone. She and I slept together for quite a few nights. For those first weeks, she was the most physically shaken of the three of us.

KIM ◆ I was 24 hours behind everyone else, realizing how bad the crash was. My siblings and friends were there to experience first-hand through the news all of the images. For me, it wasn't until walking out of O'Hare that reality sunk in: we were about to begin the journey of our lives together without Mom and Dad.

And for it all to have happened at O'Hare. I had always loved coming to O'Hare with my parents to pick up and drop off people. There was a spirit and buzz about the airport and terminals that I loved and found exciting. Walking out that afternoon, it was a sad and scary place. I was afraid to look at people or out the windows, fearing what I might see.

As we got in the car, we went to see Dad's sisters, who had flown in and stayed with Dad's nephew and his family, whom we occasionally saw on holidays. We were not close to them at all. I remember being angry sitting around a table with them and could not wait to leave. I wanted to go home! I wanted all of this to go away! I slept that night and for nights to come at Melody and Bob's. At some point in the next few days, I visited with friends at our usual watering holes on Lincoln Ave, hoping that being out with friends would make me feel better. Carol, one of my best friends since first grade, made the drive with me back to Arlington Heights and spent the night.

We slept on a pull-out sofa in my sister's family room. It was there I dreamt about Mom and Dad. In the dream, we were sitting in a booth, in a coffee shop, in an airport. Mom sat quietly at the table, but Dad was animated, explaining that we could see him and hear him, but no one else could. He got up and demonstrated walking through a door. I know other people were sitting with us, I assume Melody and Jim. The last time we all sat together in my heart. Dad told us they made it to Hawaii and were in a spectacular place. Everything was okay! They were okay. But Mom, who said very little, seemed very sad. We asked Mom about her jewelry, and Dad repeated, more than once, "Where we are, she doesn't need jewelry!

Everything sparkles where we are now." Dad was very upbeat and positive about their new surroundings.

As we were leaving the bustling coffee shop, Dad held the door for people, but no one could see or hear him. His antics continued to make us laugh. I didn't want them to leave. I wanted to stay in that dream forever.

I sat up trembling and woke up Carol, telling her I'd spoken to Mom and Dad. It's the only vivid dream I've had in 40 years of the two of them. I believe they came to me in that specific dream since I was the youngest and still lived at home. I was the one who needed the most direction. I'd called off a wedding, lost a dear friend, finished my undergraduate degree, and completed student teaching. I juggled two jobs as a grocery store clerk and a cocktail waitress on Rush Street. In my young, chaotic life, Mom and Dad were my anchors. They were the most important people to me, and now they were gone, like they vanished into thin air. No bodies to lay to rest.

Even though I haven't had a dream like that since I've replayed and relived that dream hundreds of times. It reminds me how Mom and Dad are always guiding me and our entire family. I know they've guided me hundreds of times over the last 40 years. Sitting with me, in their absence, every time I've boarded a plane. They're with me as I look out the window and count the seconds.

29.

30.

31.

SEARCHING *for* MOM AND DAD

MELODY ◆ After the weekend of the crash, we made plans for a memorial at St. Hilary's on the following Saturday, June 2nd. This would've been my sister's wedding date before it was called off. Somehow our family never canceled the church date. How odd a coincidence was that?

During the week, I fielded and made hundreds of phone calls to inform friends and family of Mom and Dad's deaths and let them know about the memorial. We decided we'd have everyone back at Mom and Dad's house after the memorial. It was a short walk from the church, and gatherings at our home were such a common occurrence. The women from the church guild Mom belonged to, along with other friends, took over the making and planning of food and drinks after the memorial, something they regularly did together after funerals.

Kim, Jim, and I got our old home ready for a party as if we were welcoming Mom and Dad back. Jim lined up people to bartend. Most important to all of us, we planted petunias down the front walkway like Mom would have done every Memorial Day weekend since building their home in 1946.

Mom and Dad met through their respective parents during World War II. Grandpa Borchers (Dad's dad) always tried to get Mom to write to Dad overseas. She didn't, but on Halloween night, 1945, Mom met him for the first time at the Northmore Tavern here in Chicago. Dad showed up in his uniform, and they were engaged less than two months later on Christmas Day. Married on Valentines' Day, 1946.

Mom and Dad definitely moved fast because I arrived less than a year later!

I always felt Mom and Dad loved one another, even through difficult times. Mom had asthma, and she couldn't do much more than sit in a chair some winters. Grandma would come and help, and Dad would get home earlier from work. There were some difficult financial times in our house, but I never felt like things couldn't be worked on and would ultimately get better. There was no quitting in our family. We believed that things would always be fine with some hard work and by helping each other out. We were always a team!

KIM ◆ Mom and Dad didn't shower each other with lots of gifts. Dad would occasionally buy Mom her favorite Estée Lauder perfume, and she'd be grateful. But after saying thank you, she'd say, "How much was that?"

They liked to give each other cards for their Valentine's Day wedding anniversary. Mom signed her card "Nudy," and Dad signed his card: "Yum! Yum!" Never got the story behind that one (not sure we wanted to, either!).

The dance floor was their happy place. They were both great

dancers, and they loved dancing with each other. Everyone loved to watch them out there. Mom would put a leg up in the air and — as you'll recall from that epic post-game Cubs celebration — a headstand was never out of the question.

Not only were they a finely oiled machine on the dance floor, but those two were masters at planning a party. Dad could polish a kitchen like no other. He loved when the copper sparkled, and he'd set up the bar and manicure the front yard. He'd do all the physical setup — tables, chairs, etc. — a day or two before a holiday dinner, Mom would have the menu written out, describing each item like we were at a restaurant. She would

Mom & Dad's
"Champagne Punch"
✳ Christmas Eve 1975

have the table set, and within every bowl, dish, or platter would be a label or description of what went in that vessel.

To this day, Melody and I do the same. We put Post-Its on bowls and platters, so everyone knows, come showtime, here's where the food's supposed to be.

Mom was the cook and the gardener, and I helped her plant and pick petunias. She passed on her love of gardening to all of us, and while Melody and Jim are the master gardeners, I still love gardening and planting flowers. Petunias are one of my favorites in honor of Mom.

One memory of Dad that set an example for me, and it's something I've reflected on throughout my life, was on Christmas Eve, 1975. Christmas Eve festivities were in full swing around the punch bowl when the phone rang. I answered and it was Dad's sister, Corrinne, who lived in Wisconsin. She asked to speak with Dad. I handed Dad the phone, and a few minutes later, he returned to the party and continued to be the host with the most. It wasn't until the following morning when he told Mom and me that his dad had passed away. That's what the phone call was all about the night before.

"Why didn't you tell us last night?" I remember asking.

"There was nothing I could do at that moment," Dad replied. "Christmas was in full swing, and I didn't want to put an end to a happy occasion. There are plenty of days ahead to mourn his loss. He lived a long life (93 years), and he wouldn't have wanted his death to stop or disrupt a Christmas gathering."

JIM ◆ Dad was always the first person up every morning. By the time he woke everyone else, he had been to Schroeder's Bakery, read the morning paper, and prepared breakfast — which usually consisted of an orange, halved and sectioned, cereal, and a sweet roll. Then we were off to the bus stop. When we were running late, Dad chased the bus down a couple of times!

Every once in a while, as a special treat, Dad would bring home lobster tails to everyone's delight... except for me! For some reason, as a kid, I decided I didn't like lobster (even though I'd never even tasted it). Mom would have to make me a hamburger or an egg salad sandwich.

This self-imposed lobster ban lasted until college...until I actually tried it. Now I know why Dad was so excited!

I still wonder how many amazing lobster meals I missed out on over the years.

MELODY ◆ While preparing for their Memorial Service, we received a call at the house from the Coroner's office. Dad had been identified! He was identified with the first group of people, including the pilot, co-pilot, and a few stewardesses.

We speculated why Dad was with this group. Mom and Dad would not have been in first class, but Dad was an engineer and knew how to fix most things. Back in 1979, the take-off was shown on screen, so passengers would have seen something was immediately wrong. Maybe Dad rushed up to the front to help right the plane. We will never know if this occurred or not, but, knowing our dad, we like to think he did everything he could to save Flight 191.

Much like he did when he saved Mom's life during Jim's childbirth. Mom ate a bag of potato chips right before going into labor. She had to throw up, but the nurses were not paying attention. They clamped an oxygen mask on her while the doctor stitched her up. A little while later, Dad was with the doctor in the cafeteria when all of a sudden: Code Blue.

"That's Nudy!" the doctor said. The two rushed back to the room.

They charged in. The nurses had Mom upside down, trying to dislodge what she was choking on. Mom was turning blue. There was no working oxygen tank, either. So, Dad sprints down to the basement of the Edgewater Hospital and finds a tank. He gets it working and brings it back to the doctor to set up for Mom. They called in a lung doctor to get the food dislodged, and he damaged her lungs, which ended up being the root of Mom's asthma.

When they had her upside down, Mom said she was reciting the 23rd Psalm in her head and thought, for sure, she was going to die. If Dad hadn't found the oxygen tank and got it working, she might have died that day.

Looking back on that phone call from the Coroner's office, we were so excited about finding Dad. We were jubilant, almost like he was coming home.

KIM ◆ You would have thought we won the lottery when Dad was identified!

Again, in my mind, I imagined his whole body was found, not possibly just a finger, dentures, or body part. We were told, by Cooney Funeral Home, that it was best we not know — or see — what remains of our parents were sent from the Coroner's Office at O'Hare.

The Cooney family knew Mom very well, they all grew up together. They were simply protecting us from the stark reality of the crash.

WE ALL NEED *to* BE STRONG

KIM ◆ I was physically sick leading up to the memorial service, and I tried to keep myself busy with little projects. I helped prepare Mom and Dad's house for the reception, and I had wallet-size photo cards made to distribute. The photo was of Mom and Dad at Christopher's (Melody's son) christening in October. It was one of the last photos ever taken of them.

I know I ordered 1,000 photo cards, and we still ran out.

To this day, I carry this picture with me wherever I go, as I know others do too. (*See next page.*)

MELODY ◆ Mom and Dad were terrific grandparents to Christopher and were my role models for grandparenting later on.

They babysat for Christopher two days a week the first year of his life. We lived in Arlington Heights and would drive to Mom and Dad's in the city, drop him off, and then head to our offices downtown. Sometimes he'd stay overnight, and we'd pick him up the following night.

Either way, we would always have a terrific dinner together.

JIM ◆ Much of the time leading up to the memorial is a blur to me. I was mostly going through the motions helping Mel and Kim to do what I could, and I mainly dealt with the house or procuring records/information.

But I do remember one night, I returned to my apartment on Briar

Place to discover my roommate, or maybe one of his guests failed to close the back door. My Irish Setter, Duffy, named after our childhood Cocker Spaniel, got out and was nowhere to be found.

This was a crushing blow. It was extremely important not to lose one of the few things I had left! I looked for four days, including one 24-hour stint hanging out in my truck on Broadway. Someone told me they'd seen a young man walking an Irish Setter with a belt as a leash. When I finally found him, the fellow was very nice. He'd been taking good care of Duffy and was about to take him to his father's house in Park Ridge. Had that happened, I never would have found Duffy again.

Finally, one tiny positive outcome amidst my devastation.

KIM ♦ It was a beautiful day for Mom and Dad's memorial service on Saturday, June 2nd, 1979. In the morning, the house was a bustle of activity. Friends of Mom and Dad's setting things up, dropping off food. Many priests congregated who were co-celebrating the Mass as well.

The dream I had of Mom and Dad came up in conversation, but I reluctantly gave details to the priests. I remember thinking this dream was so special, almost sacred to me; I didn't want to share it with priests I hadn't seen in a long time.

We all left the house together, and I can still see Susie Montoye and Mickey Gallery sitting on the front steps. They were keeping an eye on the house so we could keep it open throughout the service. The three of us walked the block and a half to St. Hilary's.

The church was standing room only. I remember my knees trembling as the three of us waited our turn to follow the priests and celebrants down the aisle. I couldn't help thinking this could have been me walking down the aisle in a wedding dress with Dad on my arm, not with Melody and Jim on either side. Jim turned to me as I was beginning to lose it.

"No tears, Kimmy. We all need to be strong."

Mom was raised Catholic in a household where her dad was Catholic, but her mom was not.

Dad was Lutheran, raised us all Catholic, and was one of the best non-Catholic parishioners St. Hilary ever had. He was always volunteering and helping wherever needed.

MELODY ♦ Mom's Catholicism meant a lot to her, whereas Dad's "Protestant faith" was whatever church they lived close to. When Dad went into the Coast Guard, he somewhat randomly wrote down "Lutheran" as his faith. He supported Mom's wishes to raise us all Catholic. Although he was a very active member, he never thought about converting. And Mom never asked him to.

In our house, values were stressed more than faith. Doing what was right was most important.

JIM ♦ Our parents' faith was not your typical "all go to Mass on Sunday" setup. We were brought up Catholic because our Mom was Catholic and the Catholic Church would only approve of our parents' "mixed-faith" marriage if their children were baptized and raised Catholic. Just the church looking out for itself... Early on, I decided the Catholic Church was all organized religious bunk (not the actual word I would use).

We all went to Catholic grade school and high school. I was an altar boy. But the fact is, we learned everything we needed to know about being a good person and doing the right thing from Mom and Dad. Period.

KIM ♦ For decades, Mom never received Communion because her first marriage during college was never officially annulled. Years later, when she was working at St. Joseph's in Chicago, Father Sebastian and other clergy counseled her and convinced her it was fine to receive Communion. It'd been so many years since her divorce and she'd spent all this time volunteering and working for the Chicago Catholic Archdiocese. She shouldn't continue to be pushed away.

Finally, with their blessings, Mom and I walked up to take Communion together. I'm sure this was a "Red Letter Day" in Mom's heart!

MELODY ◆ The actual memorial on Saturday exceeded all of my expectations. As mentioned earlier, Mom wrote me a letter four months before the crash. Father Huppenhauer, who we knew as "Wally," read her letter during the eulogy. Wally was a family friend of Mom and Dad's who actually taught me how to drive! He's the one who baptized both of my sons.

> *"I will keep getting us together as long as God gives me the strength. After I can no longer do this or yes, even after I am gone, I would like you to take the torch, my firstborn, and keep on trying to get them together, not only for the fun of it, but also for the love of it. Maybe one day not so far into the future both Kim and Jim will be married and you will have a whole gang to round up. Please remember my request and do try to comply. It will take patience on your part, but I know you can do it, Mel. I don't have too much to leave the three of you except my love for all of you and my pride in all of you and I hope that carries over to your children and their children.*
>
> *Your loving mom,*
> *Grandma Nudy."*

To tell you the truth, I don't remember exactly what I was thinking when the letter was read at the memorial. At that moment, there were too many other thoughts and things I was worried about. Bob was at the memorial with me, but Chris wasn't (he was too little. This is why we left the memorial after-party early to pick him up from the babysitter).

But I do remember re-reading Mom's letter those first years after their death, mainly because I felt like I couldn't really command people to come to gatherings. I would softly invite and hope they would eventually come. The letter helped me build up my confidence to be the one in charge of organizing. Once I got in the swing of organizing family get-togethers, I read the letter more for comfort and to feel close to Mom. I loved her passage about loving children when they're small but even more when they're older. I read the letter at most of our family gatherings on the anniversary date of the crash.

KIM ◆ We all made our way back to 5508 California Ave. If the memorial was an amazing, solemn service, the after-party was best described as a "happening." It was not somber at all. We toasted over and over again to Nudy and Bill. It was as if we were hosting a party to welcome them home from their trip!

Mom and Dad would have loved seeing their house filled with so many people whose lives they touched throughout the years, and to see these people sharing wonderful memories with us and trying to support us in our loss. I remember Dad's sister, Ellen, who flew in from Florida, commenting on the crowd of people.

"Are *all* of these people parishioners? Acquaintances through the church?"

"No," I replied, "every person here knew Mom and Dad and was a friend of theirs or involved with them through us at some point in their lives."

But still, even with all of the toasts and beautiful stories, it was hard. When I walked into our kitchen filled with all of Mom's friends, doing dishes, putting out food, wrapping up food, I remember feeling angry that Mom wasn't the one leading the charge. In her own kitchen, no less! I remember Mo Flynn hugging me alongside the house by Mom's rose bushes. I remember changing into a cooler dress up in my bedroom and secretly wishing I could just stay there and reverse time to when this would always be my room, my bedroom, the one that shared a wall with my parents. We'd often yell, "Good night!" back and forth to each other. Or, if I was tip-toeing in late, I'd whisper, "I'm home," and one of them would say, "Good night, that's good. Sleep tight." (Mind you, the next morning, Mom might have more to say about my late arrival!)

I wished I could just go to bed, wake up, and there'd be Dad, always the early riser. Even on weekends. He'd have the coffee going and, since it was a weekend, you could always count on a coffee cake with a hint of cardamom seasoning from Schroeder's on Lincoln Avenue or the Swedish Bakery, Signe Carlson, over on Foster (what is now known as Andersonville).

My friends loved sleeping over for that Saturday/Sunday breakfast. The coffee cake, the oranges, the bacon. During the week, the spread was grab and go, but Dad would always wake me and Mom up by shouting up the stairs, "Ladies, start your engines!" He'd have my hot rollers plugged in, warming up. My car was cleaned off in the wintertime and warmed up for my trek to college or work.

And you can't be in that kitchen, looking out at the backyard, without remembering one of my all-time favorite memories. Melody, Mom, and I were fixing lunch on a Saturday while Dad was out mowing the grass in the front and back. Out of nowhere, there was a *tap tap* on the kitchen window that faced the backyard. We went over to look out the windows, and Dad was streaking around the backyard! And when I say "streaking," I mean like *streaking*, streaking. It was a big craze in the 70s. It was so shocking to see! All of us were hysterically yelling. He ran so fast, I don't recall seeing much of him!

Those are the memories I wanted to hide in. But at some point during the party, officers from the Chicago Police Department and the FBI came to the door, asking if they could dust for Mom's fingerprints. So, while hundreds downstairs and in the yard gathered and partied in their honor, the officers dusted many things in our parents' bedroom to help with Mom's identification.

As they did this, I remember thinking: How come Dad was identified and Mom wasn't? Weren't they sitting together? I was sure we would know more once Mom was identified. Twenty-five years later, we learned more about the identification process, but not much.

Melody and Bob left the party early to pick up Christopher from the babysitter. The party went on late into the night. Jim and I, along with our friends, continued the "Irish wake" on Rush Street, our old stomping ground. At this point in time, I was working at Pippins and the Lodge part-time, so I knew many of Jim's co-workers and friends as well.

I have no recollection of who we were with, where we were, but I do know I woke up on Jim's couch on Briar Place near the lake. Jim and his roommate, Pat, were gone for the day. The sun was shining brightly, and there were sounds of people enjoying a beautiful Sunday morning — biking, laughing, walking, talking. These sounds ripped at my heart. "Why is the sun shining? Why are people laughing?" My world had come to a screeching halt, and I wanted everyone else's world to as well. Whether I shed a tear or not during the memorial, that didn't matter now. The floodgate of tears opened, the trembling began, and panic was setting in.

I tried dialing phone numbers I could remember. No one answered. I'm not sure why or how, but I called my girlfriend Ellen's house, and her Mom answered. I rambled and cried, and she listened to me for well over two hours. Ellen and her boyfriend, Ray (now her husband of 35 years), came home while I was talking to her mom. They offered to pick me up and drive me out to Melody and Bob's.

I was a mess, and I had no place to call home. I didn't want to be in the house by myself, and I didn't really want to be at Melody and Bob's, as it was too far away from my world of friends and happenings. Jim's seemed to be the best place, at least temporarily. I needed to be with my family.

My world had crashed into a million pieces and, for the first time in my life, I felt totally on my own and alone.

FAREWELL *to our* CHILDHOOD HOME

KIM ◆ A few weeks before their flight, Mom and Dad took me down-town to First National Bank to put my name on their safety deposit box, just in case "anything happened." I remember thinking at the time, "Why are they doing this?" I guess, because I still lived at home, they felt I was the one to put on the box.

They shared many stories that day, explaining various documents to me. They showed me the papers for Rosehill Cemetery. They said that Mom would be buried with her parents at Rosehill if anything happened to them, even though she preferred an above-ground burial in the mausoleum. She didn't fancy being buried in the ground, and it was definitely a hard No when it came to cremation.

Dad, on the other hand, actually built crematories in addition to overseeing the building of incinerators, boilers, and repairs throughout the Midwest, but mainly in the city of Chicago. Being cremated was always part of his plan. His ashes would be interred with his family at the far south end of Rosehill in the mausoleum.

"Don't you want to be buried together?" I asked.

"No!" Mom said. "We've discussed this. When the day comes, and both of us are dead and buried, we've promised to meet up with each other somewhere between Peterson and Foster Avenues on Saturday night for a drink."

MELODY ♦ I continued trying to find legal documents. I also looked for Mom's jewelry, but we never found it. We figured she must have taken it all with her at the very last minute. We never got anything of Mom's returned to us, but a year and a half later, I did receive a few of Dad's things by surprise in the middle of a workday. I was a paralegal working downtown in the First National Bank Building, and one day a female representative from American Airlines showed up and asked for me. I came to the reception area, and she handed me an envelope that held Dad's wedding and signet rings. Just like that, handed it over. I asked if there were still items at a warehouse in Texas that hadn't been distributed yet, but she knew nothing and said sorry. I have no idea what her position was with American.

This was the only contact we ever had with American Airlines. We never received a letter, call, or any correspondence of condolence; nothing as simple as, "Sorry for your parents' deaths on our aircraft." We had multiple correspondences with the insurance company for the airlines, but these interactions were far from warm, fuzzy, or caring.

But let's go back in our story to early June 1979. On June 10th, almost two weeks after the crash, Mom was finally identified (maybe the fingerprints collected at the party helped after all). She was in one of the last groups of people physically identified. There were many people, I was told, who were never physically identified, but through their ticket and not showing up elsewhere were identified en masse.

KIM ♦ Just like we did with Dad, we reacted as if we'd won the lottery. Mom was also released to Cooney Funeral Home on Southport Avenue.

Melody and I picked out a gold oriental long jacket/dress that Mom loved and had worn to a few dressy occasions. She had a passion for Asian-style clothing and furnishings, even wearing fancy chopsticks in her French knot. I was probably the only kid in my neighborhood in the 1960s who would venture to Chinatown with their mom to go dress shopping. Mom often said she felt like she had been of Asian descent in another life and made chop suey once in a while, but nothing that knocked your socks off. Chinese cooking was not at the top of her list of delicious meals she cooked and served.

Those Chinatown outings were more about the clothes than the food. For special occasions, she was a fan of the Mandarin collar-silk jackets. Those were more readily available in Chinatown compared to mainstream department stores.

We brought the gold dress to the funeral home, envisioning she'd at least be covered in one of her very favorite outfits. To this day, I often wonder what parts of both Mom and Dad were in their caskets. But when I think about it, I prefer to imagine them sort of vanishing from this world, together, floating up to heaven from the crash site.

On Wednesday, June 13th, there was a brief prayer service at Cooney's, and both caskets were at the front of the parlor, side by side. Dad's coffin was draped in an American Flag honoring his military service during World War II. There were no framed photos as it wasn't something people did at the time. We had no involvement in the choice of caskets. We think American Airlines simply reimbursed the funeral home for the caskets.

It was so devastating to see their two caskets side by side. There were minimal people in attendance, just family for a brief prayer service at the funeral home. A much different event compared to Mom and Dad's true service and "wake" back on June 2nd.

JIM • My memory of the caskets and Cooney Funeral Home is very hazy, at best. There's so much I've blocked out from the time of the crash until many years later and, even then, many things still remain a blur.

When we asked to see their remains, they strongly suggested that was not a good idea. I guess they were trying to spare us or protect us. Grudgingly, I went along with Mel and Kim and did not insist on seeing what they had. My personal opinion was there was probably nothing left to identify except for teeth. Keep in mind they were in a fully fueled DC-10, plunging into the ground. Basically a giant bomb. Everything other than some metal was exploded and incinerated on impact.

Regardless, I still wish I had gone with my initial instinct. My only solace is knowing their end was virtually instantaneous, other than a few seconds of terror. My hope is maybe they had a chance to look into each other's eyes.

KIM ◆ We proceeded to Rosehill Cemetery to bury Mom in the "new" section, north of Peterson Avenue, next to her mom and dad. Dad's remains were cremated per his wish, and we would return in a few days to inter him in the mausoleum at Rosehill. Mom's burial was followed by a luncheon at Grassfields, a popular place on the north side where Mel and Bob held their rehearsal dinner.

The luncheon is a blur to me. What haunted me throughout this entire day was the reminder that I was never able to see Mom and Dad to say goodbye. Everything felt so distant and sped up, and this funeral was another layer of pain and stress in my being.

On Friday, June 15, 1979, the three of us returned to Rosehill Cemetery's Mausoleum with our Aunt Pat to place Dad's ashes in a vault where his immediate family was and would be buried. He was interred at 10:00 am. As hard as it was to try and enjoy lunch after those events, we wanted to keep Mom and Dad's love of food alive. Food and Red Letter Days go hand in hand, whether in a restaurant, a picnic grove, or home kitchens.

MELODY ◆ Years ago, Kim made a wonderful collection of family recipes with pictures and some of Mom's handwritten notes on the event - who was there, what was served. While writing this book (*Safe Landing*), Kim and I always recaptured some of our family's favorites. Ham Salad brings back memories of Mom grinding the ham with pickles and mayo for the lunch we would bring to our annual school picnic. "Chicken Mornay," always made for Kim's birthday, was a special recipe of Mom's. Our family still loves her chicken parmigiana, spaghetti and meatballs, and little pizzas for appetizers. Oh, and fish! We had lots and lots of fresh fish that Dad would pick up from Burhops downtown. Red snapper. Turbot. Cod. Perch. And occasionally, like Jim mentioned earlier, delicious lobster.

Dad had his special business lunch spots near the Loop. His Number 1, I believe, was Martini's, where we would occasionally go for a special dinner. As kids, we were exposed to many restaurants in the city and even Sieben's Brewery on Larrabee.

The list of restaurants and spots in the city where Mom and Dad loved to go could go on and on (we've actually included a list in the back of the book). We highly recommend looking over this list, checking which ones are still around, and then creating your own food and drink tour around Chicago!

June, 1979

KIM • Not sure when I officially moved in with Jim and his roommates, but I hosted a pre-graduation party on Briar for a few NEIU fellow grads and friends the following Monday before heading to my college graduation. That night, Colleen, Cathy, and family attended the ceremony. Afterward, we had appetizers and drinks at Hilary's in Water Tower Place to celebrate. This was a very bittersweet night and occasion. We all tried to be happy and celebratory, but we were only going through the motions. My first "Red Letter Day" without either of my parents was heartbreaking. It didn't feel like these occasions could ever carry the same amount of joy.

A few times a week, I would stop in and pick up the mail at Mom and Dad's house. Sometimes friends and I stayed there if we were out late in the neighborhood. Either way, day or night, it didn't seem right to be in my house of 23 years without Mom and Dad.

The three of us, along with our Aunt Patty, Mel's husband (Bob), and baby Christopher, decided to gather at 5508 for a traditional BBQ on the 4th of July. Saddest and worst 4th of July ever. The house had a musty odor from being closed up. The backyard was overgrown, and it was a blaring reminder that Mom and Dad were gone. I don't think we all stayed very long before going our separate ways.

Even being together was becoming difficult at this point. Our roles were changing. It was a far cry from our other 4th of July celebrations, especially our epic family gathering for the Bicentennial celebration not too long ago on July 4th, 1976.

MELODY • Weeks went into planning the Bicentennial celebration. We had the usual buffet of food and drink. Moscow Mules. Oh yeah, plenty of Moscow Mules! But there was more family present and a more than usual number of friends of family and neighbors.

We played games and held a 4th of July parade in our own yard at dusk! I was dressed as the Statue of Liberty, and Kim was Betsy Ross. Everyone was dressed in red, white, and blue, singing the Star-Spangled Banner and carrying sparklers. The yard and house were decorated with lights and red, white, and blue decorations — it was magical and fun!

KIM ◆ Towards the middle of July, as I'd been doing since June, I stopped by our parents' house to pick up the mail. When I put my key in the front door, the door opened but only as far as the inside chain lock allowed. My heart started to race. This meant the door was locked by someone inside.

I looked through the small opening allowed by the chain and saw Mom's big school bell in the middle of the living room floor. Normally, it had a prominent spot in the back den. Someone had either broken in and left, or they were in there right now!

I rushed next door to the Pysters. Ruth Pyster called the police. I used her phone to call Melody and Jim, and Mel took a taxi from her work downtown. Jim arrived with the police. Not only was this a robbery, it was most likely a group who broke in, vandalized, and broke things. The TV was smashed on the floor in the den.

"I hope whoever did this got injured trying to steal the TV," Jim said.

It was determined they broke in through the back basement window. The house was torn apart, and we didn't know precisely what had been taken since we'd been treating the house more like a museum — not to be touched. Never in a million years would we have thought to run some sort of inventory in case of a robbery. That thought never crossed our minds with everything else going on!

We decided to pack up and take anything of real value left in the house. This horrific event added insult to injury and set the wheels in motion to sell our anchor, our base, at 5508 N. California Ave.

Such a raw day of emotions. We felt angry and sad, but maybe most of all, we felt sheer disbelief. This began the gut-wrenching (and back-breaking) project of clearing out our childhood home, a place where our parents had lived for over 30 years.

JIM ◆ It seemed like every item I picked up conjured up another memory shared with Dad. Things I dearly miss now, such as the seasonal chores performed by just the two of us: taking down the canvas awnings and putting up the storm windows, cutting the grass, learning how to operate the in-ground sprinkler system, which at the time was very "high tech."

The front stairs triggered memories of playing little league baseball

all summer long. I would wait for Dad to come home with our mitts and ball so we could play catch on the sidewalk in front of our house.

Cleaning out the garage, there was the tool bench — my favorite classroom. Dad taught me to use tools and repair all types of things. Anytime something needed fixing around the house, he would take the time to show me what tools were needed and how to use them. Later, when I was out of the house in my own apartment, Dad would drop in out of the blue, and we would go to lunch frequently at Berghoff's downtown, a favorite of mine to this day.

I loved putting up the outside Christmas lights on the shrubbery and windows leading up to Christmas. Anyone who knows me will not be surprised that I still have those light sets. I can picture putting up those lights with Dad like it was yesterday! I used to love the fact that you could easily pick out our house during the holidays as we were the only ones with Christmas lights for blocks in either direction. The Christmas season following the crash is when I started decorating the outside of my bar, The Lodge, with lights and garland. I did this by myself as my own way of continuing one of my favorite holiday traditions.

But the event I looked forward to more than gifts or Christmas tree decorations was setting up the Lionel Train. Dad bought this for me way before I was even aware of what a train was. Each year we added a new car or apparatus to the layout.

Those memories are indelible and wonderful. Wow, how I miss all of those moments with Dad!

MELODY ✦ Dad and Jim's train set was the first holiday item that went up after Thanksgiving. The train's cars were large, as was the whole set-up. It was situated on a ping pong table and remained up until the end of January. Jim had a conductor's hat and sat on a stool to run the train. Kim and I got to play with the train, but Dad or Jim was usually with us if anything went off the tracks. Also, worth mentioning, Kim nor I ever wore the conductor's hat!

The train did not just go around in circles. It had cars that delivered milk and a coal car that picked up coal, just to name a few. Plus, there was smoke that puffed out of the engine too. My birthday is at the end of January, so we needed the basement space for my birthday parties. Otherwise, the train might have stayed in place much longer each year.

KIM ◆ We sold the house to Pat, which felt nice because we knew their family. Pat's brother, Billy, was Jim's best friend throughout grade school. We knew he would take good care of our childhood home.

On Saturday, October 6th, Pat and Eddie moved in. I stopped by 5508 to get a cardboard storage drawer container from the front hall closet. It was the last time I walked up those stairs and backed out of the driveway onto California Avenue.

SHOWING UP

KIM • In October, we handed over the keys to the new owners of 5508 N. California. I moved into my first apartment in West Rogers Park. It was a stone's throw from where I went to high school and it was not far from my neighborhood and familiar surroundings. I was decorating and adjusting to my apartment, living with a good college friend, Cathy. Ready or not, a new chapter of being on my own was underway.

Even though it was a great apartment with an extra storage room, I was not emotionally stable enough to take on this responsibility. But, at the time, this was my best and only option. We decorated the space with many items from Mom and Dad's. And I remember trying to be happy, trying to look happy, trying my best to act happy and be OK. But I was not OK. I was still in shock, fighting depression, loneliness, and every stage of grief. So much had happened in just four months. The death of Mom and Dad. Their anything but ordinary burials. Never getting to say goodbye. Pair all that with college graduation, the burglary of our childhood home, moving twice, and then saying goodbye to the only home I had ever known. This was more than I could handle. Especially in my early 20s.

As the holidays approached, the stress and anxiety of facing the Red Letter Days without Mom and Dad were becoming a reality. Melody assigned me an appetizer and sweet potatoes. Everyone always loved Mom's sweet potatoes, but I never ate them. Somehow, someway I made the sweet potatoes and picked up Aunt Patty to take to Mel and Bob's. But it didn't feel right. Mom cooked the sides. Dad picked up Patty. Not me. Roles kept changing.

That Thanksgiving was tolerable. We went through the motions and since Mel and Bob had hosted Thanksgiving before, it wasn't totally out of sync with Thanksgiving pasts. We all showed up and tried doing our part, but it was a forced gathering.

Christmas was certainly not the *Ho! Ho! Ho!* holiday gathering we all looked forward to every year. We all showed up at Mel and Bob's on Christmas Eve with hopes of giving Christopher a Merry Christmas with gifts and all. Melody jumped into her leadership role given to her in Mom's letter, but her family room seeped water, and my chicken livers cooked into a pile of floured livermush. We got through the night even though our hearts were breaking. We longed for California Avenue. We longed for the old roles and familiar traditions.

Leading up to Christmas, Cathy and I hosted back-to-back parties for family, friends, and even former neighbors at our new place. When the drinks were flowing, the music blasting, and lots of people around, it was a great way to escape the pain of this first Christmas holiday — if only for a few hours!

The parties continued with a New Year's Eve that was over the top. I guess we were all kissing '79 goodbye in a big way. Mel and Bob met me and Jim for a drink early in the night. Dressed to the nines, Jim, his roommate (Pat), and I, plus some more of Jim's friends took a limo to a fabulous party at a home on the North Shore. I even wore one of Mom's Asian silk jackets for the occasion.

MELODY ◆ Our first family get-together after the crash (that wasn't related to memorial services) happened in July for my son Chris' second birthday. I remember having a small party for him with kids in the neighborhood, and then a big party for family members and friends. I tried to do what I thought should be done, but it wasn't easy, even with the laughter and smiles of a darling two-year-old boy.

Bob and I celebrated our 10th wedding anniversary with friends.

But I continued to push Bob away. I didn't want to ever hurt again like I was hurting from losing my parents whom I loved so deeply. I thought the answer was not to love someone that much ever again. Luckily for me, Bob hung in there with me and my family. It probably helped that he had been a part of our family for some time and loved both Mom and Dad, Kim, and Jim. We continued into the holiday season, first with Thanksgiving where we had the usual family members attend but tried to mix it up by inviting other friends and neighbors. We thought it would help mask that Mom and Dad were not there, but it was even more apparent. The first time I'd made a turkey was the first year of our marriage when we were living in Columbus, Georgia near Fort Benning. Bob was in the service and I was making Thanksgiving for both of us. Mom had sent me a detailed letter entitled "Let's Talk Turkey," which took me step-by-step through the whole preparation of the Thanksgiving dinner.

Currently, I would say I'm a pretty good cook. But let's just say that first dish I put on the table in 1969, well, Bob said it was tasty, but the spoon stood up on its own in the container. He was wondering what it was and I told him it was the gravy! The only other time I had hosted Thanksgiving prior to this was when our Grandma Ryan was dying and Mom couldn't do it but she, of course, helped me make the gravy, potatoes, etc. But now, at this first Thanksgiving after their deaths, it hit me: I'm responsible forevermore to get this family together. At that moment it was incredibly daunting.

As Kim shared earlier, that first Christmas was also at my house and it had its own quirks. It was an extremely warm Christmas Eve and it had constantly rained for a few days. Our family room flooded and all of us spent time mopping it up. I guess it kept our minds off the constant reminder of who was not there and why we were in Arlington Heights and not at California Avenue in Chicago. Thanksgiving and Christmas of 1979 were the beginning of many difficult holidays and family gatherings. But we kept on doing it.

I learned early on that I could invite and give dates and times, but other family members might be there on time or hours later. I wasn't Mom and couldn't demand them to come. Or be there right on time. I just hoped they would and most of the time they did. We kept on celebrating to the best of our ability, all those Red Letter Days without Mom and Dad.

KIM ◆ From January 1980 to June 1980, much of my routine was sleeping a good part of the day, working on Rush Street, and partying all night. Mind you, somehow, someway with a gaggle of angels looking over me, I drove many times when I shouldn't have. This destructive pattern of behavior continued for me until the summer when I took a teaching position in the NW suburbs. Again, I had not dealt with all the grief and stress of the crash and as much as I loved teaching, it was not the right time for me. Everyone thought that getting a "real" job would get me back on track and would solve my problems and then I would be OK. But I was still not OK. Trying to be super teacher, super party girl, super coach, putting on a good face, all collapsed on Bastille Day, 1981. I was hosting a party at the apartment, and I remember looking in a mirror and admitting to myself: I need help.

Numerous times leading up to this moment I drove out to Mel and Bob's wanting to ask for help, but when I got there, I always ended up telling them I was OK. I didn't want them to worry about me.

From September '81 to the spring of '82, I finally got help. Alison, a good friend of my brother's (who I had also become friends with) put me in touch with the most fabulous therapist in the Chicagoland area: Dr. Neal J. Gordon. Six days a week, I made the trek to Oak Park, a side of the world I was not familiar with for sessions to talk, to journal, to get back on track. Neal helped me find myself again and focus on all the things that mattered to me. He helped me heal and begin living again, building relationships again with family and friends. Mind you, even though I was struggling with the demons and pain of Flight 191, I still somehow managed — along with Jim and Mel — to gather for Red Letter Days, birthdays, and special occasions. I have no recollection of what we did on the first anniversary of the crash, but I do remember sobbing my eyes out on May 25, 1982, en route to see Neal. All of 1980 and much of 1981 are a blur. It was a bad dream I wouldn't wake up from until the summer of 1982.

Williams Bay, Wisconsin, 1980

MELODY • The couple of years after 1979, life continued to happen for all three of us, but it was forever changed, different, and difficult. Personally, I felt I was the most fortunate of the three of us because I had Bob and my son, Christopher, to get me up and out of bed every morning. However, at the time I remember going through the motions of living and doing without feeling.

In 1980, I was pregnant but not feeling well. My first pregnancy was a breeze and I worked right up to my due date. Even delivery was relatively easy, which was surprising since it was done naturally, plus it was a breech birth. But this pregnancy was different. I almost lost the baby at 3 months. Then, at 5-1/2 months, I went into labor. Bob was out of town on trial and I called our friends the Murphys to come over as I was not feeling well. Mike Murphy stayed with my son, Chris, and Vera Murphy drove me to the hospital. There I delivered a dead baby and baptized him Robert Stanley. I chose the name Robert because Bob had told me that we didn't need another Robert, two was enough in the family, he and his dad. Stanley was the name of the doctor who delivered the baby.

After Mom and Dad died, besides the emotional upheaval of my life, I felt my body had physically changed too, and not for the better. Experiencing this pregnancy validated to me that I was physically different.

Prior to delivering this baby, Bob and I got back to looking at larger houses in Arlington Heights. We had been looking prior to Mom and Dad's deaths, but this project was put on hold in 1979. We did put an offer on a house in early fall, 1980, but lost it in a bidding war. I feel like that loss was a precursor to losing a child two months later.

The one highlight in 1980 was Jim, Kim, Bob, and I taking the money we got from the sale of Mom and Dad's home to purchase a home in Williams Bay, Wisconsin, a block from Lake Geneva. We decided we needed a family home to gather, and not just at my home in Arlington Heights. We'd vacationed and done day trips there with Mom and Dad years ago and decided it was an easy distance for us all to get to. This was one of the best purchases we ever made. It launched our 15-year Lake Geneva vacation residency; allowing us to get together year-round but especially spring through fall for Red Letter Days. We also scheduled the summer season so all three of us could have our own weeks alone or with our friends. Bob bought a boat and the healing for our family began primarily at this new location.

Late 1980, I started feeling a little more normal again about Bob, myself, and my surroundings. In February 1981, Bob and I were successful in buying a house in Arlington Heights and we still live there to this day. I also became pregnant again in March 1981. The beginning of this pregnancy was better than last time but not as good as my first pregnancy. At the 7-month mark, we were down in El Paso, Illinois visiting our Army friends, the Hagemans, when all of a sudden I started bleeding. I was taken to their hospital in nearby Bloomington via ambulance. The next day, my doctor back home decided I should be taken via ambulance back to our local hospital Northwest Community. I was there for a week given steroids to strengthen the baby's lungs in case I was going to deliver soon. Instead, I delivered Jordan on his due date December 15th. But I was on bed rest for the last two months of this pregnancy while my mother-in-law came every week and stayed to help take care of Christopher, Bob, and me.

Throughout our grief recovery, my in-laws were always accessible and calm. They never judged or commented on me or any of the family as we struggled through these first few years after the crash. They were the best and I couldn't have asked for more supportive and loving in-laws and grandparents. Again, I was fortunate to also have these two people to rely on along with Mom's sister (Aunt Patty). These three individuals (along with Bob) put up with me, supported me, and loved me while I was navigating these various phases of grieving. By 1982, they helped me start to care about all the beauty of life that I still possessed - my family and dear friends.

KIM • By August of 1982, I was in therapy 5-6 days a week trying to find myself. During this process, I decided to try to get back to teaching — which was my passion — and move away from bartending downtown. On a particularly busy Friday afternoon, a waitress showed up at the front service station of the bar to work that day. She was very nice and in between orders I shared with her that I was hoping to find a teaching job in the next few weeks. She told me there was a job opening at a Catholic School, St. John something, she thought, north of downtown, somewhere near Western Avenue. After that conversation, she disappeared. I figured the manager had moved her to a different bar or room as the Hangge-Uppe had two floors and multiple bars.

The next day, I got out the phone book and started looking for any St. Johns in the area. On Monday morning, after calling numerous schools, I called St. John Berchmans on Logan Boulevard and the principal answered the phone. I explained how I was hoping her school had this job opening. She was surprised by my call since she had finished her last interview for a 6th-grade position but had not publicly advertised this role. She asked how I knew of the opening and I explained that someone I met thought there might be one. She told me if I could be at the school in an hour she would grant me an interview. I pulled my hair back into a bun, threw on a skirt, and somehow found the school. She hired me on the spot!

When I was working at The Hangge-Uppe the following Wednesday, I casually asked someone, "Hey, who was the girl working happy hour last Friday?" But there was no record of any girl working that particular shift. It was so bizarre. To this day, I have no doubt in my mind that she was an angel, sent to guide me down a good path. I would later find out that a good friend of my Aunt Patty's went to mass and prayed for me every day at the church where I would restart my teaching career. "We don't meet people by accident. They are meant to cross our path for a reason." It's a wonderful life!

The best person I crossed paths with at St. John Berchmans was a junior high history teacher named Peter Jockl. When we met, I was focused on getting back to teaching and rebuilding myself, not looking for love or a relationship. But life is filled with expecting the unexpected and meeting Peter was just that. We loved to cook, entertain, teach, and enjoyed each other's company. We made a great team. He was willing to be part of gatherings and outings with my friends and family. We met in 1982. Engaged in 1983. Married in 1984 at St. John Berchmans. I never considered getting married at St. Hilary's where I had grown up as it would have simply brought back too many memories, which I was still not ready to face. Our wedding was filled with sunshine, happiness, pure joy and celebration with Melody, Jim, and those I loved. It was the first big joyful Red Letter Day celebration for the three of us since the crash. Even good friends of our Mom and Dad were part of the day. I have no doubt my parents hand-picked Peter for me from above.

Looking back on those years from 1979 to 1982, there was so much pain and grief, but also this steady, gradual recovery. How we survived and kept going is a miracle in itself!

GOING THERE: OUR JOURNEY BACK *to the* CRASH

MELODY ◆ There's no playbook on how to handle death and all its encumbrances when people die suddenly in a plane crash.

When we started writing this book, we realized just how big of a gap there was between the immediate aftermath and us "going there" in terms of trying to honor our parents, honoring everyone on the flight, and aiming to create some type of memorial for everyone who lost a loved one on that terrible day. When I say "big gap," I mean over 20 years. Almost like our lives hit the fast forward button from 1979 to 2001.

And maybe that's normal. A plane crash isn't something you get over quickly, and the stages of grief don't happen overnight. Plus, there was family, and work, and school. There was always something going on. So, I'll try to explain our big time gap and why I think it took us so long to begin planning some type of memorial. But, in the end, I think the best explanation might just be that there is no playbook. We took exactly the amount of time we needed to move forward.

I was the keeper of most family crash memorabilia — notes, newspapers, programs from memorials, sympathy cards, etc. I initially stored these in a legal file since I worked for a law firm and my husband was a lawyer. That was the world we knew. As more things were collected from people giving us items, plus our family's notes and correspondence with the airline insurance company, I moved the items to a box and eventually a large plastic container.

All the while, I was not really re-reading the newspaper stories. My attention was more on my parents' estate files. My husband helped with legal matters like our parents' house sale and anything else where we needed a lawyer's advice and/or signature. I had things to do handling our parents' estates separate from whether we were filing suit against the airlines or settling. Bob and Jim together went to see aviation lawyers.

So, this file/box/container was active for the first couple of years but not directly concerning the newspapers and information about the crash. Reaching out to other families wasn't really on our radar either. At times, I thought about contacting the family of Eileen Plesa since she was from our area. I did end up calling once, not knowing if it was the correct Plesa family. The phone rang and rang, and no one answered. There was no answering machine either. And that was that. I didn't pursue it any further. I thought about contacting the family of Judith Wax, one of the Playboy Magazine writers (several of their writing staff was on Flight 191) after I found out we shared the same hairdresser in Lincoln Park. But there was always so much to take care of, and, honestly, it was still too painful to bring myself to call. If they did pick up, what would I even say?

Years went by, decades went by, and it felt like there were our day-to-day lives on one side of the room and this container of documents on the other. Maybe we subconsciously knew how much energy and emotional effort it would take to "go there," to open up the container and bring Flight 191 back into our lives in more than a legal document/procedural type of way.

It wasn't until a few months before the 24th anniversary when Kim and I were ready to open the plastic container and really look at its contents.

KIM • Melody and I met on a Monday in July to open a container of yellowing newspapers. We finally had the courage, strength, and willingness to look at these articles that had never fully been read, only glanced at and tucked neatly away following the crash.

We began compiling lists — lots of lists. Lists of passengers, crew, journalists, photographers, emergency personnel, and key facts. We found ourselves sidetracked by all these facts that had somehow escaped or faded away from our memory. It's obvious now that we blocked all of this out because it was far too painful to face these physical reminders of the heartbreak we felt.

Once we had the lists of people and events, we sat down at Mel's computer together. For the very first time, we typed in: American Airlines Flight 191.

Wow!

Tons of sites appeared, but none allowed us to connect with others who had lost someone on the flight. Remember, this was pre-Facebook, so any social connection online was still kind of the wild west. We checked website after website. We were attracted to the site about the "Spirits of Flight 191." I think it was reading about the "spirits and sightings of Flight 191" that catapulted our quest to visit and find the site where our parents and 271 other people lost their lives, in the air and on the ground. We felt we needed to visit the crash site and ask the "Spirits of Flight 191" to guide us in our journey to properly honor and acknowledge their lives lost at the 25th anniversary.

We ended our first session by contacting Fink Memorial Park. This was a park built in Highland Park by a father who had lost his son, Michael, on the flight. We were saddened to hear that Michael's father had died a year ago but that the Highland Park District would attempt to locate his family for us.

At this point, we realized that many of the people connected would be gone since 20+ years had passed since the tragic event.

My son (Jimmy) and I left Melody's home in Arlington Heights. We followed a map from the Tribune and drove by the area we were pretty sure was the crash site of Flight 191. Our hearts sank as we saw what we would later confirm: construction on the site/within the debris field of Flight 191.

I immediately called Melody. Had we waited too long? Could the field where our parents lost their lives be part of the O'Hare Expansion? Why had we waited so long!?

We decided to make some phone calls. Maybe the bulldozers off in the distance were not the site of the crash. The brother of a friend of mine told us we needed to contact the Chicago Police Canine Division of O'Hare, located on Touhy Avenue. After many attempts, Melody finally connected with Officer Fortuna.

In the meantime, I composed letters. The addresses were a total crapshoot, and many were marked "return to sender." But we kept trying. I began my letters with, *"I'm not sure if you are the Mrs. Dillard who lost a loved one on Flight 191...."*

At first, Officer Fortuna was elusive. He wanted to know how we came upon his phone number. But, eventually, he allowed us to visit the land behind the canine training grounds, as long as no media came along. Oddly enough, my son actually went to school with one of the police officers from the Canine Unit.

With yellowed newspapers in hand, my Mom's charm bracelet on my wrist, and my Dad's bow tie in my pocket to guide us, Melody, Jim, and I arrived at a dilapidated sign identifying the Canine Unit. From the sign and overgrown foliage, it sure didn't look like a working facility.

We were wrong. Officer Fortuna greeted us amicably and opened the gate. From there, Mel, Jim, and I walked at least two to three blocks west and then north on a fairly dense grassy area until we came upon a very high fence.

Approaching the fence and walking through overgrown brush, attempting to see something through the high chain-link fence, left me feeling empty. I had been so afraid to look for so long, and now that I was here, it wasn't scary. Just an overgrown, rundown field. Instead of fear, this experience incited a numbness throughout my body. A feeling of sadness and disappointment that our parent's remains, and those of all who had died in this spot, were literally forgotten without any care given to their "burial ground" and no sign or marker indicating the lives lost beyond the dog training facility and fence. Melody and I both said, "Mom is not happy here." We need to let her know, and Dad as well, that we are here to begin a journey to try, in some way, to make things right for them and the other 271 individuals. We couldn't fix what had happened, but we were going to try to find other family members who lost a loved one and make sure they were not all forgotten in an overgrown field.

Walking along the fence, Melody and I knew we were heading down a path of search and discovery of which there was no turning back.

JIM • Driving home that day brought a ton of thoughts and memories to mind. There are so many snippets, streets, and locations that remind me of traditions with Dad. Memories that, at the time, were taken for granted. But I think, maybe starting on this day, and definitely ever since, these memories make me recall Dad and smile.

Like driving down Lake Shore Drive, although he never said as much, I think it was one of Dad's favorite routes. He would explain how the reversible lanes worked. (Years ago, Lake Shore Drive had cement curbs in the middle of both northbound and southbound lanes that would rise hydraulically out of the roadway, magically transforming the lanes to six in one direction and two in the other reversing for the evening rush hour).

Driving down Clybourn Street makes me immediately wonder what Dad's take on the changes and development would be. Forty years ago, it was an empty corridor with nothing but factories and industry.

Dad spent a lot of time driving in and around the city as a salesman. He was also the family chauffeur, driving our friends and us virtually everywhere. He knew every shortcut to get anywhere in Chicago. He was a great driver, but faster than our Mom cared for! Within several months of purchasing a new car, the paint on the passenger side of the dashboard (at that time dashboards in a car were entirely made of steel and chrome with no padding), would be worn down to bare steel by our Mom's practice of putting her foot up to brace herself for the coming collision that never materialized! He also taught us to drive probably sooner than would have been considered proper.

Dad was a great teacher.

MELODY • And a great coach. In 6th-8th grade, I was involved in track and field through my parochial grammar school in the city. We would participate against other Catholic and public schools, and then a big meet was held at River Park in the city. I was tall in 6-8th grade (never really grew much after that), and I ran and participated in the high jump. Dad not only built a high jump in our backyard with sand, but he also showed me how to do a scissors kick to jump over. I did pretty well after his coaching!

Dad was also a good tennis player. He wanted me and Jim to learn tennis. In the 1950s, tennis wasn't that popular with kids, and if you could find a tennis court, usually it was in disrepair. However, Dad would take Jim and me out to the court, and he'd teach us the strokes and how to serve. Frankly, I remember being bored by the whole thing, I think Jim was too, so then Dad would say:

"Okay, you don't want to play. I guess I'll play by myself."

Then he'd have us sit along the side while he volleyed back and forth to himself while jumping the net. It was a pretty awesome sight. He'd come back over to us.

"Alright, do you want to play by yourself or together?"

Jim and I would then be more attentive and try harder.

Dad finally got his tennis player later with Kimmy. However, as I got older, Bob and I played and joined tennis leagues in our 40s. Whenever my family went on vacation, tennis was always part of our activities with Bob and our sons. Now I have a granddaughter playing tennis in high school. Dad must be smiling!

KIM ◆ Back in 8th grade, I tried to replicate Dad's jumping over the tennis net move...but I fell and broke my arm. What a way to kick off the school year!

A few years later, Dad taught me how to drive. To this day, I often repeat his mantra throughout those early driving lessons:

"He who hesitates is lost."

In other words, don't be afraid to go. Make decisions. Keep a good speed, because those who go slow cause many accidents.

Twenty-four years later, we weren't hesitating anymore. We were willing to go forward by looking back, facing our fears, and taking steps to accept what happened, to find out more about what happened — not in a newspaper — but from people who were there. No more looking away. As Dad would say, "Full speed ahead!"

We thanked Officer Fortuna for his help and proceeded to visit the trailer park that rims the area of what we believed to be the crash site. We met Kandice Kramer from the Oasis Mobile Park, who shared her stories from the day the plane crashed. She took us to the back of the park to look down on the place our parents and 271 others died.

Along with others we met throughout this very long day, she seemed to think the site would be used for water runoff and that the project was overseen by the Department of Water Reclamation for the City of Chicago. As luck would have it, a classmate of mine from grade school was sitting as the President of the Water Reclamation Department. I got his home number from a friend and teasingly asked him (Terry) if what we were told was true.

First official visit to crash site, 2003

"Are you going to put my parents at the bottom of the Elks pool with the runoff?"

From this point on, I knew if we could gain access to the fenced-in crash site, Terry was the key.

Terry forwarded my email to individuals who were in charge of the land. They agreed to honor his request and make arrangements for me, Mel, Jim, and our spouses to get out to the site. By the time the date was

First official visit to crash site, 2003

set, we had found Michael Lux, the son of Walter Lux (the pilot), and Mrs. Dillard, the wife of co-pilot James Dillard, and asked if they wanted to join us. Terry, knowing my background, asked if we would like a priest to join us, and, of course, I answered yes!

In my email, I let him know that we just wanted to place a flower on the site and let our parents know we are going to try to do something that should have been done by someone...25 years ago...but better late than never.

As has been the case throughout this Flight 191 journey, individuals who cross our path and help us out are often connected to us in some other way. We made our first "what a small world" connection when we boarded the bus for the first time to head out to the site. While making small talk and introductions with Father Mike Zaniolo, the Chaplain at O'Hare, we found out he grew up within blocks of our house and attended St. Patrick High School, the same school where my husband attended, and my son Matt was currently going. Father Mike has been our support and spiritual leader from that first visit to the site, to the Dedication, and again at the 40th anniversary.

Official visit to the crash site of American Airlines Flight 191
August 21, 2003

"To live in hearts we leave behind is not to die."

All of us here today are a living testament to this quote today. Pilot Walter Lux, Pilot James Robert Dillard, Nudy & Bill Borchers and all of the other 269 passengers, crew and those on the ground....do live everyday in our hearts and have for the past 24 years.

I'm sorry that it has taken us this long to finally stand, pray and connect spiritually with those whose lives were taken here May 25, 1979. You see, at the exact time Flight 191 crashed, taking the lives of my parents, Pilot Dillard, Pilot Lux, and all on board and on the ground, it sent all of us, the families of those on board, and those connected with the flight in some way, into a tailspin, up into the air emotionally, with the task of putting broken hearts and dreams back together...attempting to land safely ourselves, emotionally...

Today, as we stand on and near the crash site...we have landed safely..a small group of loved ones of Nudy, Bill, James, and Walter, but we leave here today with the hope of connecting with many more loved ones..to celebrate all of the 273 lives and spirits of Flight 191 this coming May, 2004, the 25th anniversary of the flight.

I thank God, Terry O'Brien, Joe Zurad, James Glowa, the City of Chicago, the Department of Aviation, and Father Mike for helping us finally stand together on this hallowed site, giving us the opportunity to pray for all whose lives were taken here...It is my hope that they have found eternal peace,

That the road did rise to meet them,
That the wind is always at their backs,
That the sunshine is warm upon their faces
The rain falls soft upon their fields
And until we meet again,
May God hold them in the palm of His hand.
You all live on in our hearts and will never be forgotten..Amen

Love,

Kim

MELODY • Father Mike Zaniolo said a prayer, Kim read a reflection, and we dropped 273 rose petals. Mrs. Dillard left a bouquet of flowers as well. We were also able to take soil from the site.

After experiencing this powerful moment ourselves, we knew we had to get other families out here on the 25th anniversary. We wanted families to have a chance to join with other people connected with the crash to begin to share and heal together.

Kim and I asked if a memorial service could be held in the chapel at the airport, along with a chance to meet everyone after the service and then be bussed out to this crash site. They agreed it could be done.

But how to get in touch with all those people 25 years later? That was still our challenge, and we already had a sense it would not be easy. Again, there was no Facebook, and the internet, as we know it, had just really started. So, we started working off the passenger lists from the newspaper 25 years ago, which were sketchy at best. We knew our parents' full names were never listed in the paper, so we doubted the accuracy of most of these lists.

We contacted both the American Airlines CEO and Community Relations person to acquire an accurate list of passengers (aka the official manifest). However, they continued to put us off. They said that on the actual 25th anniversary, the list would be released to the public. Obviously, that would be too late to help us locate people and send out invitations. Fortunately, with the help of Michael Lux and his contacts at the airlines, we got a better list than what was in the newspaper. It wasn't the official manifest, but it put us on the right path in our search for families of victims.

We also tried contacting any journalists who wrote articles 25 years ago, but we never heard back. We contacted Playboy Enterprises, as they had lost a few of their writers and executives in the crash, but they never responded. We contacted Oprah with no results. We contacted names we could still find in local telephone books with limited success. We left many messages on answering machines that may or may not have been to the right people.

But anytime we contacted someone connected to the flight, we were thrilled. We contacted local fire departments, and their chiefs said they'd put out notices to any of their current or retired members who were involved in the rescue of the crash.

The search continued. We received the help of another friend of Kim's, who just happened to be a private detective. During his free time, he helped pursue a large group of people from the Momence area in Illinois and was somewhat successful.

But as the anniversary got closer, we had only been able to connect with about 15 families, and half of them were hesitant to attend. We understood their pain, knowing the intense suffering of so many of us, even 25 years later.

This journey had been a heartfelt experience and an eye-opener. Through the efforts of Chaplain Rev. Zaniolo (who is also a pilot) and Michael Lux, we made connections with many American Airlines employees who never had a chance to properly grieve for their friends. At the time of the crash, they were told by American to carry on business as usual. I think because American Airlines' stance towards us at the leadership level had always been in an adversarial role, we hadn't thought about their airline employees. These employees had worked with the people who died. These were their friends.

We heard stories of a stewardess who was part of the Flight 191 flight crew the last month. She'd flown in with them at 1 PM but was not flying back in the afternoon as someone else had taken her place. By the time she got to her car, she saw the flames and knew it was them.

We heard about people in the trailer parks who were immediately impacted by not having easy access to their homes, mulling around, trying to get on the site through their boundaries. For these people, even 25 years later, hearing a low flying airplane conjures up tense feelings from Flight 191. We also encountered helpful people like Gail Dunham, a former stewardess, who started NADA/F (National Air Disaster Association for Families). She assisted us in trying to connect with other people. She encouraged us to get this memorial done and then a marker placed somewhere in the future.

We met with an aeronautical reporter who was writing a book on what actually caused the crash of Flight 191. His book would be told through the eyes of maintenance people from American Airlines. Their view was that American had cut the time for proper maintenance of the DC-10s. We listened to him and, though fascinating, we were more interested in our memorial that was happening in a couple of weeks. There was also a television show detailing the cause of the crash, fittingly titled *Why Planes Crash*. The blame was placed solely on American Airlines due to the shortened maintenance practices of their DC-10s. Thankfully, this show didn't air until after the memorial. I believe it would have caused much anxiety for some participants and might have disturbed this event coming together and its overall healing purpose.

Our goal was to carry on with a positive attitude. We didn't want to slam American Airlines or dwell too much on what caused the crash, or what could have been done better, or whatever other, "if only..." scenarios might arise.

We contacted newspapers to get our story out and to help us reach more families, but no one was interested. At least not until the day of the memorial. At that point, they wanted to be in the chapel with us. As I explained, this memorial was not a publicity event. This memorial was an opportunity for people who lost loved ones, or helped with the recovery, to mourn and share with others. They never had a chance to do this, so in our eyes, outsiders and media were not welcome. We needed press or publicity before the actual memorial, more as an announcement, to help gather more families to the event.

KIM ◆ In addition to our efforts to find people, our Flight 191 spiritual guides always seemed to put people in our path to help us. One of those people was Joe Boisso, a father I sat next to at our son's basketball games. He took it upon himself to find family members connected to the flight. He spent many a day off combing through the library and local papers in the town of Momence, Illinois. Many lost on the flight worked at a publishing company located in this town. They were headed to a book convention along with other writers and those connected to the literary world.

About a month before the actual 25th-anniversary gathering, I was sitting at a baseball game, cutting out tiny colorful strips of all the names from an array of passenger lists. Another parent asked what I was doing. I explained my project and found out she was related to one of those injured on the ground! Her husband's cousin was nearby the crash and suffered severe burns. It was another incredible coincidence to find someone directly impacted by the crash. We reached out to invite him to the 25th. But, understandably, due to the trauma and injuries he experienced on that day, he was unwilling to attend or be part of this gathering. I often think of him and how his life changed in so many ways because of Flight 191, a memory he lives with every day. I pray that he has been able to block the horror of that day from his memory.

I wanted to make sure stories like his and others were properly recognized. It was important to me to have a resolution of remembrance and recognition of this disaster from the City of Chicago read out loud at the event. What I assumed to be a routine, easy request was definitely not. The Mayor's Office thanked me for my request and was sorry about the accident, but stated they could not help at this time. After trying a variety of communications — phone, letter, email — I reached out to Alderman Pat O'Connor, with whom I attended grade school, and he also knew my parents. Pat had actually called me during the reception following our parent's memorial service, asking if he could be of assistance in any way. I remember thanking him for his call and saying we didn't need any help. Twenty-five years later, we definitely needed his help. His office said they would see what they could do.

Alderman O'Connor was able to honor our request. At the City Council meeting prior to the 25th anniversary, the resolution was read and approved, recognizing Flight 191 as the worst non-terrorist aviation disaster in the history of the United States. The resolution honored the memories of those who died, those who were injured, and those who responded to the crash on May 25, 1979. Having Flight 191 publicly recognized was one of the many highlights of something that was so overdue.

With 20 days to go, we found another relative of someone lost in the crash. I sent out a personal letter, excited to share what we had planned for the 25th anniversary. Finally, it felt like things were coming together.

MELODY ◆ The actual Flight 191 Memorial Service took place at 12:30 pm at the O'Hare Airport Chapel on May 25, 2004. A declaration was issued from the City of Chicago, honoring the 273 people who died. People then could linger and talk in the Fellowship Room next to the Chapel.

At 2:00 pm, those of us who wanted to visit the crash site were taken there by O'Hare personnel. We sprinkled all 273 names around the site. Those of us who wanted to were given plastic bags to gather soil from the site, and Rev. Zaniolo joined all of us in prayer.

As I stated in the Chapel and again in an article for NADA/F: "There was no policy in place 25 years ago for family members to meet each other. We just did not know how to do it. We hope to continue to hear from other family members from Flight 191 as we establish a website and hopefully a memorial marker. A place where victims' families can go and have some quiet reflection. A memorial helps as we move forward together."

This is the short speech I gave to all of those in attendance on the 25th anniversary:

25th Memorial Anniversary/Crash Site 2004

"Recently someone asked me, 'Why are you now doing a memorial?' I am sure a psychologist would have many reasons. My simple reply is that we now are comfortable sharing and going there. For the last 10 years, my sister and I would talk about planning a memorial and reaching out to other families. We would say, 'Well, let's plan on the 25th anniversary,' probably because it was off in the future. But when the 24th year grew near, we knew if we did not do it now, we may never pursue this dream.

This journey of putting together a memorial has been a heartfelt experience and an eye-opener. This crash obviously affected the families of those who died, but the effects of this crash were farther reaching than I had realized.

And then there are all of our stories and that is what today is about, for us to share our memories of our loved ones with one another in the fellowship room and out at the site. As just as each one of us carries a memorial in our hearts of our loved ones, we feel it is important to pursue a permanent memorial marker honoring the 273 individuals who lost their lives because of Flight 191. Hopefully, O'Hare and American Airlines will assist us in this pursuit and find an appropriate place.

Today we obviously do not have a plaque in place, but we do have some tangibles such as the posters with the names of all who were lost on Flight 191, thanks to Michael Lux, to take and leave out on the site, and the cut-up passenger lists so that we can all sprinkle their names on the ground and we can bring back with us some of the soil from the site where our loved ones last rested. Before we adjourn to the Fellowship room, please make sure to sign the guest book, and we hope that there is someone in this group that might be able to develop a website so that we may communicate with one another with the hope of finding more families. Again, thank you for making this journey so fulfilling and for coming today to keep the memories of our loved ones alive."

Those individuals who crossed our path and helped us in a small or big way were recognized in the 25th-anniversary program.

KIM ✦ As over 50 individuals took in the crash site, I could hear an occasional, "There's my dad's name," "There's my mom's name," amongst a hushed gathering. People dug up dirt, prayed, and reflected on this sacred ground where so many died. At the time of takeoff, we gathered as a group for 31 seconds of silence, led by Father Mike Zaniolo. He blessed the crash site and sprinkled holy water. As he led the group in prayer, a plane passed over as if letting us know the spirits of Flight 191 approved of our ceremony, knowing we had never forgotten them.

It was a very emotional day for all who were present. We vowed to find a place to hang a plaque that Flight 191 would always be remembered.

FINISH *the* FLIGHT

JIM ◆ Within a year after the accident, I decided to go to Hawaii to see one of my best friends from high school, Tom Juliano. Tom had moved to Honolulu after high school. I stayed with him for a week, and Tom being the perfect host, showed me a great time. I fell in love with Hawaii. And, in retrospect, I think my first trip there so soon after the crash was me trying to complete Mom and Dad's trip.

Years later, I was introduced to Jennifer by a friend at the Lodge. Shortly after that, she began working at the Lodge, and we started dating. The first trip Jennifer and I took together was to Hawaii. By then, Tom managed a hotel in Maui that we stayed at and had a fabulous time. In retrospect, I realize that for a very long time, I coasted at work, through relationships, girlfriends, and to some degree with Mel and Kim.

That began to change when I met Jennifer in 1990. She was somewhat younger than me and I guess she was okay with my ambivalence. She was not necessarily looking to settle down. Eventually, Jennifer and I moved in together. For me, that was the beginning of my coming to terms with my loss and the realization there was a reason to move on. Jennifer saved my life. After being a couple for many years, I finally proposed when we were driving home from a Chicago Bears game.

Once we decided to get married, Hawaii seemed like the logical and perfect place for our wedding. I don't think we realized until later that our wedding would coincide with the 25th anniversary of the crash. As the date approached, the significance of this became more important to Melody, Kim, and me.

KIM ◆ I was thrilled to hear Jim and Jen were getting married but a bit taken aback when they said, "in Hawaii." As teachers, my husband and I didn't have a special nest egg marked "Hawaii." But come "hell or high water," as our parents would say, I was determined to make sure not only me, but the 4 of us — Pete, Matt, Jimmy, and I — would be on the beach to witness this grand event with everyone else.

Their wedding closely followed the 25th anniversary of Flight 191, taking place in late summer 2004. I also felt like I was finishing Mom and Dad's flight. The first notes for what would later become this book were actually scribbled on a piece of paper while waiting to take off. I wanted to capture the moment of how I felt looking to my right and left, front and back, seeing my sister and our families buckling our seat belts on an American Airlines flight. I counted the seconds our parents were in the air as we taxied down the runway and prepared for lift-off. It was one of those surreal moments you will never forget and marked another key moment of us moving forward as a family.

I remember telling Mom and Dad that we were okay and we were headed to Jim's wedding to a gal they'd love, and can you believe it, it's in Hawaii! We are finishing your flight and have no doubt you will be with us all in spirit!

MELODY ◆ I was still on a high from us doing what Mom would have wanted, recognizing all 273 people who died together on American Airlines Flight 191 at the 25th anniversary. And now, going to our brother's wedding three months later, in Hawaii, with our entire family, wow. We were finishing Mom and Dad's flight. It was the ultimate Red Letter Day for our family!

Getting everybody to Hawaii wasn't easy. Jordan, our youngest, was a senior at the University of South Carolina and was already off at school. But we arranged for him to come for the rehearsal dinner and wedding, and then he flew back to school prior to all of us leaving.

That's one thing Mom and Dad certainly instilled in us; Red Letter Days are not optional! We made sure the whole family was together for this event.

We chose to fly American Airlines. Jim and Jen did not. Forty years later, they still have never boarded an American Airlines flight.

KIM ◆ The entire trip, festivities, ceremony, parties, and all were filled with genuine laughter and fun in a paradise setting! We snorkeled. We did the Road to Hanna. Pete and Jimmy flew to visit Pearl Harbor. The rehearsal dinner, wedding, reception, we crammed so much into those five days we were there.

The morning of the wedding was really special. Just the three of us (there were over 80 people, friends, and family who made the trip to be part of this "Big I Do") met to have a quiet moment, burying one of Mom's hankies and one of Dad's bow ties in the sand. This was our way, in a sense, to have them physically with us on such a Big Red Letter Day. It was very emotional. The three of us were together on the beach where they were headed. Our feet planted firmly on the ground, united, together. Without a doubt, we had landed safely from all the grief, the turmoil, the angst, and trauma from losing our parents on Flight 191. Hugs and tears were exchanged, and we headed off in different directions as we had the whole day to enjoy before their 5:15 PM vows outside cottage F, their wedding suite.

MELODY ◆ We weren't sure if Jim would join us to bury Mom and Dad's items on the beach. We didn't want to make a big deal about it either if he didn't want to.

Much to our surprise, he joined us. It was significant that Jim joined us in this burial, as recognizing Mom and Dad were long dead was still difficult for him. Kim and I seemed more at ease with their deaths, especially after working on the 25th and listening to other people's stories that seemed much worse than ours. In fact, we realized we were much better off emotionally than many of the other families who'd lost loved ones on Flight 191. But that day, I felt we had all come full circle. We were all in a good place, and when we buried their items on the beach, we all felt that in some way, we had finished their flight and knew they were really with us.

JIM • My memory of the items buried on the beach is faint, but I knew I needed to be there with my sisters, making Mom and Dad part of my wedding day. It was a special way to begin my wedding day by remembering and reflecting on Mom and Dad with Melody and Kim. In our minds and hearts, we had completed their flight.

KIM • Jim, being the groom, had lots to do.

But for me, Melody, and our families? Hey, it was time for some fun!

Melody, my son (Jimmy), and I met Jen's niece, Emily, to float along the shore at the far end of our resort to see the turtles who everyone said gathered along the rocks below the surface of the water.

To make a long story short, Emily, Jimmy, and I, supported by a long foam noodle, decided to float with our arms hanging over the noodle, with our faces looking down through the water at the turtles and ocean life below. We had front row seats to Maui's breathtaking ocean life below the surface. As we enjoyed the view of the world below, unbeknownst to us, and in a very short amount of time, we had drifted far from the shoreline! Melody had kept an eye on us, and I realized we were in a bad situation seeing her waving for me to come back in with the kids.

One noodle. No life vests. This was not good...

I stayed calm while Melody, Bob, and Pete (who had now joined her), ran to the hotel for help. Thank goodness, Robin Love, who was a roommate of Jim's when I lived with him on Briar Street, her date for the wedding was a former Navy Seal. They immediately swam to the three of us floating on that noodle at least two city blocks out from shore. I could no longer see the bottom and stayed focused on keeping Jimmy and Emily calm and happy. Robin's Navy Seal date had Emily get on his back, and Jimmy continued to hold on to the noodle as Robin and I each took an end and swam him to shore.

JIM • The wedding was everything we could have hoped it would be. Our good friend, Kathy Britt (Bryant), who has lived in Maui for over 30 years, was invaluable in helping us organize the logistics of planning the wedding.

My toast was to thank everyone who had made the long trip to share in the event. I thanked Jennifer's parents, Joe and Peggy, for their generosity in helping us make the wedding happen and to point out that the only people missing were Nudy and Bill, who would have had such a great time.

We tried our best to party hard, as I know they would have approved.

KIM • Even though Jim cannot remember what he said, Melody and I will never forget his toast. It was the first time he publicly recognized that Mom and Dad were not with him, or all of us, on his Red Letter wedding day.

Marrying Jen, who had been his soulmate for many years, was to me and my sister his way of moving forward and embracing life, love, and the possibility of a broken heart again. For the first time in 25 years, the three of us all seemed to have landed safely and reached a good place in our lives. Ironically, all of this happened in the very place where Mom and Dad were headed on May 25th, 1979.

I know in my heart they were with us that magical week in Maui.

MELODY • As much as we were aware of the significance of our families flying on an American Airlines flight to Hawaii 25 years after our parents' doomed flight, we would find out a year later the significance of Jim and Jen's choice of wedding venue.

While organizing papers and notes in my basement, I came across a scribbled note that I immediately knew was from my notes taken during my last phone conversation with Mom the day they left for Hawaii. This note depicted all the resorts and locations they were going to stay for their

25th   Waiki   Hilton Hawaiin
26th   Village
27th
28th
29th   Kauai   Coco Palms
30th

31th   Maui   Royal Lahaina

1st   Kona   Keau Hou
                 Beach Hotel

3rd   Helo   Naniloa
                 Surf –

3rd   Waikiki
                 Los Angeles

10-day second honeymoon trip. Coincidentally, Jim and Jen both spoke of the good feeling they got when scouting locations for their wedding at the Royal Lahaina. As you can see from this note, it was one of the locations Mom and Dad had planned on staying.

This only enhanced the memory of Jim and Jen's wonderful wedding in Hawaii. We all felt, when we buried Mom and Dad's items that day on the beach, that in some way we had finished their flight for them. We all knew they were really with us.

PERMANENT MARKER

KIM ◆ Having gotten through the 25th anniversary with success, our good intentions of keeping the momentum going, finding more people connected to the flight, and moving towards a permanent marker were sidelined by the busyness of everyday life.

My husband and I were busy juggling our teaching careers and all the commitments raising boys in junior high and high school. In 2005, I actively pursued an administrative position within Chicago Public Schools. With no formal experience as a school administrator, this was not a slam dunk by any means. I was preparing to head back to my 21st year as a Chicago Public School teacher in Little Village when I received a text from a colleague who instructed me to drop off my resume at Decatur Classical School in Chicago. Divine intervention — or as I like to say, "Mom intervention" — played a role in alerting me to an Assistant Principal position at Decatur Classical.

By day's end, I had delivered my resume to a school I had never heard of, even though it was in proximity to where we grew up and attended high school in Rogers Park. One week before school started, I moved my belongings and began my administrative chapter at Decatur Classical School. I was thrilled to have this great opportunity; to be part of the leadership team of such a gifted, high-performing school.

MELODY ◆ During the 4-5 years after the 25th memorial, life provided us with many Red Letter Days; some in celebration and some in remembrance.

Three of my now five grandchildren were born from 2007 to 2009. These children changed my life dramatically, and all for the better. I knew I wanted to help and be a part of their lives, and I'm happy to say that happened. They continue to be a significant part of me and my husband's lives to this day.

But with life comes illness and death. We lost my mother-in-law and my sister's father-in-law during this time. Also, my husband was undergoing treatments for cancer.

Like all of us, the yin and yang of life happen.

But we kept honoring Mom and Dad. Every year on May 25th, Kim, Jim, and our spouses would commemorate the crash date by going to the chapel at O'Hare. Fr. Mike would say a mass and remember all the crash victims. We would then go out to eat and remember Mom and Dad and all the fun Memorial Days at their house, bringing pictures and telling stories.

Periodically, we were contacted by families who heard about the memorial and, of course, were sorry they had missed it. We were thrilled when contact was made with another family, but meeting was difficult as we could no longer get back onto the crash site. Kim would send them some of the soil we'd collected at the 25th memorial and include that day's written program. We told them they could meet us at the chapel on the following year's anniversary.

Kim and I continued to talk about a permanent memorial, but how and where were big question marks. The idea of us just doing a plaque with all of the crash victims' names was our best interim thought. However, there were obstacles to whether the airport would allow a plaque, even though Fr. Mike said he would try and talk to the right people about it. More importantly, we still didn't have an accurate passenger list of names. We still had never received the official manifest from American Airlines!

From the beginning, American Airlines was not there in any way for our family, and I suspect it was the same for all the other 272 families. All of our communication was with the insurance company. As I've stated before, we never got so much as a call back that yes, Mom and Dad were on that plane, nor a letter saying something as simple as, "We're sorry for your loss," or, "Here are some tips on how to deal with loss of life when it happens via a plane crash." We were left to figure this out on our own — and there was no Google to turn to either.

If American Airlines had gotten families together immediately at the crash site, there would have been the realization and confirmation that yes, this is where 273 people died. We would have shared that initial shock with other families. We would not be looking for the crash site 24 years later. We would not be trying to get an accurate list of 273 people if American Airlines had tried harder to put together the names from their lists before the flight, at check-in, or by attaining records from travel agents. They probably never had an actual complete manifest of passengers for Flight 191.

When people look at our story today, I'm guessing they say, "We would not have allowed this to happen," or, "We would have demanded something more be done." Well, you have to keep in mind a few things. We were dealing with the sudden death of our parents, and there were no bodies, and no death certificates. Everything was all under federal aviation control. So, from the start, we had no control. No help on how to deal with any of this. We had no idea what was supposed to be done. If it hadn't been for my friends — one a cop, one a lawyer for another airline — I don't know who would have told us to bring their dental records where and when.

So, from the very beginning, American Airlines was on one side, and we were on the other. I didn't initially dwell on American Airlines or hate them for their lack of communication. And certainly, throughout the years, my family and I have flown American many times due to practical reasons of cost and time of flights. But while working on the 25th, that's when we developed a sort of hatred for American Airlines. This is when we learned from a journalist about the shortsighted American Airlines board meeting when they decided to cut the maintenance of their DC10s in half for money considerations. This was why Flight 191 crashed, a faulty DC10. It was hard to turn the other cheek once we knew this information.

But even with this revelation, Kim and I didn't want this negativity to poison the 25th-anniversary event. We didn't have time to dwell on it either. Besides, there are more employees at American Airlines than one board room and, as it turned out, many of them were at the service. These

folks had nothing to do with the DC-10s. They were simply coming to mourn their fellow employees; again, something American Airlines didn't do for their own people.

So, here's what I'll say, because I don't want to detour too far on this topic. My disgust with American Airlines ties back to their corporate culture. How could they not recognize this crash? And knowing their

poor maintenance decisions led to their plane crashing, that will always sting and feel like everything could've been prevented. I understood on an intellectual level how American Airlines didn't want to be associated with crashes and loss of life — not good for business, not good for the brand — but there has to be a more human solution than what we experienced in the aftermath of Flight 191.

KIM ◆ For those anniversaries following the 25th, there was maybe a mention of the crash on page 10 in the newspaper. There might have been a mention on the news, and of course I would hear from some of those we met at the 25th. They'd say, "We really need to get together again!" They all expressed a need to pursue a memorial of some kind to acknowledge those lost on Flight 191.

Whether gathering at the O'Hare Chapel or getting together for a Memorial Day Weekend picnic, what remained constant was getting together on May 25th. By doing this, we were honoring Mom and Dad and, in our own way, letting them know we would never forget them.

MELODY ◆ In 2009, my sister and I talked about how we wanted to honor Mom and Dad for the 30th anniversary. We decided we would take our family, now numbering 17, to Rosehill cemetery. We'd introduce them to their grandparents and see where they were buried - Dad in the mausoleum, Mom in her family plot. Kim and I also decided we would attend mass at the O'Hare Chapel.

Everything was proceeding like any other year, but then, to our surprise, we were contacted by the Daily Herald, the Chicago Tribune, and Vince Gerasole from CBS. The Daily Herald said a woman had contacted the newspaper in her effort to make contact with us about Flight 191. The reporter at the Herald also told me she wanted to do an article on the 30th anniversary of the crash. I said nothing was being done except my sister and I attending mass at the O'Hare chapel.

I contacted the woman connected to Flight 191. She and her family met my sister, brother, and me out at the chapel. She and her brother had lost their parents on the flight when they were very young, and she really didn't know a lot about their deaths. Again, sharing our mutual losses was healing for all of us. We talked about a permanent memorial but told her it would be an enormous undertaking. Location and names of people involved were still a problem, along with trying to locate other families. We said we would stay in touch. Kim gave her and her brother soil from the crash site and the programs.

The article in the Herald was good. It covered the crash, our involvement in the 25th, and the frustration of not having a permanent memorial. The article in the newspaper stated a need for such a memorial.

The Vince Gerasole interview took place along the fence of the Oasis Trailer Park overlooking the crash site. We talked about our personal experiences on the day of the crash and our involvement in organizing the 25th-anniversary memorial. We expressed our frustration with locating families 25 years later, as American Airlines still had not made public the official passenger manifest nor recognized the need for a permanent memorial.

Kim and I were happy about the attention being shown to Flight 191 and the need for a permanent memorial. We had not solicited this publicity, and, to my knowledge, this was the first time other sources talked about such a need. More and more people realized that Flight 191, the largest loss of life in the US (other than terrorist crashes), should not be forgotten.

JIM ◆ Being Memorial Day and knowing we were commemorating the 30th anniversary at Rosehill Cemetery with the entire family, I decided to honor Dad in a special way and inform the whole family of his military service. I still regret how we never really talked about what his duties as a "Motor Machinist Mate" on board his ship during the war entailed.

Rosehill Cemetery, 30th Anniversary, May 2009

In retrospect, that void of so many questions and conversations we never got around to led me to learn as much as I could about LSTs (Landing Ship Tanks). LSTs are the large transport ships with huge front doors in the bow that would drop an anchor off the stern and then beach the bow so they could off-load their cargo: trucks, tanks, and troops. The crew would then pull the ship off the beach by using the anchor dropped offshore.

I had ball caps made commemorating Dad's ship and service for the 30th memorial at Rosehill Cemetery.

Speaking of Rosehill Cemetery, another tradition I have adopted is honking my horn anytime driving past Mom's gravesite at Rosehill on Peterson Avenue. This tradition requires an immediate explanation if anyone else is in the vehicle.

KIM ◆ We saluted Dad in the mausoleum, wearing hats depicting his military service and placing American flags. We honored Mom at her graveside with petunias and headstands. We shared stories about them, how they met, and why they were buried in separate spots. Jim explained more about Dad's military service during World War II.

Ten years later, at the time of the 40th anniversary, I was contacted by a former student of mine who'd been serving as the tour guide at Rosehill Cemetery since the mid-'90's. She wanted me to know that when she conducts the Mausoleum tour, she speaks about our Dad and the Flight 191 disaster. She asked me why our mom is interred in a separate section. I shared the whole story, including their plan to meet for drinks somewhere between Peterson and Foster. My former student started to include this aspect of Mom and Dad's story as part of her tour.

The day ended with a family lunch at the Fireside Inn, celebrating the spring birthdays and simply being together.

MELODY ◆ During the summer, Kim and I were contacted by Kate Novich from MSNBC under the guidance of Lester Holt, a news commentator, who was producing shows on various plane crashes. The theme was "Why Do Planes Crash?" and Flight 191 would be highlighted in one of their episodes. They said they wanted to humanize these technical depictions with the people impacted by such crashes.

So, in late October 2009, Kate Novich and her technical crew came to my house and interviewed me and Kim in my kitchen. I remember Kim arriving dressed in Halloween colors as the holiday was soon approaching.

KIM ◆ Mom and Dad went out on their first date on Halloween, 1945. They met at the Northmore Tavern upon his return from military service. Mom always talked about how great Dad looked in his uniform when she met him. They were engaged on Christmas Day, 1945, and married on Valentines' Day, 1946. I guess you could say holidays were part of their DNA, and that was something that carried on to us.

So, decking the halls, decorating for Christmas, going all out for birthdays, and yes, arriving for an interview with MSNBC straight from school dressed in Halloween colors, that's just part of the territory as Bill and Nudy's youngest daughter! Being a teacher allowed me to dress and decorate not only at home but at school as well!

MELODY ◆ Kate asked about the day of the crash and dealing with the consequences. I remember telling her it was not easy and a learning experience I would not want to repeat. No one helped us on what to do and how to do it, certainly not American Airlines.

We talked about the years leading up to the 25th anniversary. We also told her our urgent need to connect with others who lost loved ones and addressed the need for a permanent memorial marker.

The interview went well. This was another opportunity to highlight the crash and continue our campaign for a permanent memorial. Kim and I both felt our journey to attain a permanent memorial site was far from being over.

KIM ◆ The 30th anniversary came and went, and the attention given to the crash did likewise. My life continued to be consumed with the juggling of family, friends, and work commitments.

Planning a permanent memorial and/or doing something special for the 35th, or the 40th after that, I expected Melody, Jim, and I would continue to work on these projects mixed in with the everyday busyness of our day-to-day lives.

But what I never would have expected was how in 2009, a group of 6th graders at Decatur Classical School would become the unlikely heroes of our story.

SIXTH GRADE HEROES

KIM ◆ To set the stage, 2009 was my 5th year as the Assistant Principal at Decatur Classical School in Chicago. The 6th graders at our school participated in something called "Project Citizen," a national civic education program coordinated by the Constitutional Rights Foundation of Chicago. Project Citizen allowed students to look at issues in their community, analyze public policies, and try to make a difference.

Prior to 2009, 6th-grade classes had researched and presented on various topics. An example of one of these projects in the past: "Why juvenile organ donation should be allowed in Illinois," inspired by the loss of a classmate to cystic fibrosis. Focusing and researching a specific issue, engaging with experts in the field related to the project, building cases as to why a policy should change, and working as a group provided experiences for students to carry with them throughout their educational journey.

Late October 2009, Melody and I were interviewed in her home for the MSNBC documentary, "Why Planes Crash" (remember my Halloween colors?). I'd left school late morning, and when I came back, I was walking down the hall when someone asked me to join in a class discussion held by the 6th-grade teachers, Beth Allegretti and Marianne Sharping and both 6th-grade classes. They were discussing the focus and direction their Project Citizen would take this year. With the prompting of the teachers, I shared how my life dramatically changed on May 25th, 1979. I explained how my parents, along with 271 others, were lost and forgotten with no memorial or place for their loved ones to gather and remember them. This was a story some of them had heard about or seen when the Vince Gerasole interview aired the previous May.

I shared with the students how my sister and I had just taped an interview with MSNBC. In the interview, we reiterated our hope for a memorial to happen someday.

Once again, timing is everything in life, and our dream became their focus. The students chose Flight 191 and the need for a public memorial as their class project.

I supplied them with artifacts related to the crash — such as newspaper clippings and articles. I shared stories about our journey finding people for the 25th anniversary and which names we'd found so far who were connected to the flight in some way. But other than sharing those artifacts and our story, I was not involved. This was 100 percent the students' mission.

The students researched every aspect of the crash, set up a website as part of their project, produced a documentary, and looked into the possibility of a variety of memorials, whether physical or something online. They started an online petition to gather support for a memorial and created a letter-writing campaign to inform officials and media outlets. They believed if they contacted enough people, something might materialize.

Periodically, they would run to find me in the school and ask me questions like, "Did you know that American Airlines received 25 million dollars from the US government for Flight 191 and none of it went to a memorial?" or, "Did you know why the plane crashed?" Those and many other questions brought back memories I tried not to think about or focus on for my own mental health. I must admit, I had no idea about the $25 million and was sick to my stomach hearing this fact. But, at the same time, I was glad the students had uncovered this through their research.

The students also interviewed people at the school who were connected to the flight. They interviewed me, my sister, and the security guard who responded to the crash. The father of one of the 6th-grade teachers was Lieutenant Joseph Locallo. He spent months after the crash helping in the identification process at O'Hare. A good number of individuals connected to our school were also connected to the flight in some way either as a first responder, family member, or simply a Chicagoan who vividly remembered that awful Friday in May of 1979.

These students reached out and investigated every aspect of the crash. They made every effort to find families, first responders, and those connected to or lost on the flight.

These 60 smart, enthusiastic 6th graders, led by teachers, and a school that allowed them the opportunity to participate in such a project, were the manpower we had always needed and never could have imagined the stars aligning in this truly unexpected way.

MELODY ✦ I remember thinking it was nice they were taking this on as their project and that more light would be shone on Flight 191 and the need for a permanent memorial, but I really didn't expect a permanent memorial to actually happen.

I held these doubts until I was interviewed by these 6th graders. Kim had always told me about the gifted students attending her school and how this 6th-grade class was exceptionally bright. I saw it first hand during my interview. They were very advanced, and their questions were just as on point as the professionals who had interviewed me a few weeks prior from MSNBC. I left that day thinking maybe they really could get the ball rolling on the permanent memorial...

But then again, what was the likelihood that a group of 6th graders could take on the political climate of Chicago to get a memorial site? Or how would a group of 6th graders go up against American Airlines and secure an official manifest? The chances felt pretty slim despite how bright and determined they were. I wasn't going to get my hopes up...

KIM ✦ As the students' presentation approached (around the 31st anniversary), an article appeared in the Chicago Sun-Times questioning why there was still no memorial.

Unbeknownst to the Sun-Times' writer, Flight 191 and the need for a memorial was on the mind of 60 very determined 6th graders in Chicago.

Leah H.
Decatur Classical School
7030 N Sacramento
Chicago, IL
60645

American Airlines
4255 Amon Carter Blvd. MD
2400
Forth Worth, TX 76155

Dear American Airlines,

"There were a few images from that day that I'll never forget."
- Paul Marcotte, "Daily Herald" reporter (Retired)

If you are like me, you have traveled many times across the country and around the world. You have witnessed firsthand all of the numerous, sometimes ridiculous, security checks before strolling through the terminal to board your flight, occasionally one of American Airlines, the company I am addressing now. However, there was a time where people did not even consider the maintenance of a commercial airplane. There is one event in particular that I am referring to;

May 25, 1979. Emergency vehicles rush to the scene to rescue any survivors that they can find. Sirens scream and wail as they dash to the site of Flight 191's crash, a gigantic fireball of burning metal and singed flesh. There is nobody to rescue. All 271 passengers, including flight crew and pilots were killed, along with 2 civilians on the ground. Following this horrible tragedy were a myriad of laws and investigations to find out what was responsible for this and how it could be prevented in the future. However, were you to search throughout Chicago, the city in which this incident occurred, it would seem as though this event had never happened, for there is no memorial that the victims of Flight 191 can go to.

It is a fact that American Airlines Flight 191 is, to date, the worst aviation disaster in all of America's history, and as I previously stated, it sparked endless safety precautions. If you want the most obvious statement towards why there should rightfully be a memorial mounted somewhere in Chicago, it is of pure common sense: it is quite frankly nonsensical that America's worst aviation disaster does not have a memorial. Family members of the victims were not the only ones whose lives were changed forever. As you can probably imagine, bystanders and witnesses of the incident have not been able to erase the nightmarish memories since that day. They will never forget the sight of that giant plane going up, the deafening sound of the engine racing off of the wing, and finally the aircraft lurching to the left until it finally plummeted into the earth, sending up an "ominous black cloud." I am appalled that you at American Airlines have not cooperated in the slightest bit when it comes to a proper service for this tragedy, and, if anything, has only hindered the progress of getting a small memorial service in 2004 which was held by my vice principal, Kimberly Jockl, whose parents both died in the crash. "When you lose somebody in any of these situations, you never get to say goodbye," she stated in one interview. To this day, Mrs. Jockl still wishes and hopes with great passion that you can at least contribute to the pay for a full scale memorial.

And now we must come to the part where everything comes together: the law. It says clearly in the section concerning aircrafts that was created by your plane crash that there is to be a memorial service and marker, paid for at least in part by the company responsible, as well as counseling for those who were changed forever, neither of which has been put into effect, even after 31 years. So if you really think about it, since there has been practically NO participation in the receiving of the rights that everyone involved deserves whatsoever, could this possibly mean that your lack of actions towards Flight 191 is escaping the law itself?

I conclude now with the hopes that you understand how much this cause means to me and my fellow classmates. We are all astounded by your near denial of everything that happened when it comes to the crash of Flight 191, and the indecent respect you were and still currently are showing the people whose families were on that plane. If you understand the urgency of this letter, show that you understand by answering to all of those who will never forget the day that Flight 191 fell from the sky.

With all due respect,

Leah H.

Example of letters

written by students

MELODY ◆ The presentation/competition date was scheduled for May 28th, 2010, at the Federal Courthouse in Chicago.

Kim invited Jim and me to attend. The students had a limited time to present, and the judges would rate theirs against other schools. I had no idea what would be judged: the project content, the presentation, the research, all of it?

The students entered the room looking very professional. But there were 60 of them! I wondered what that many students could do together in two minutes.

KIM ◆ As the school's Assistant Principal, it was challenging for me to keep my distance from a project inspired by my story and an event that changed every aspect of my life forever. I purposely kept my distance as I wanted to remain an inspiration, not a hands-on participant.

As the students began laying out the pictures, information, and such for their presentation board, I did offer them a large roll-up map that I was given by executives at O'Hare when we ventured out to the crash site in 2004. I thought my siblings and I would never use this as it was an aerial map of the runways and crash site, but this became the background of their presentation board.

I remember thinking somehow, someway, I need to be at this presentation to represent all the families like us who wanted a memorial or a place to remember and gather, but for whatever reason did not have the time for such an undertaking. Mom's voice was telling me - You, Melody, and Jim need to be there.

Melody picked me up at 9:00 AM that Friday of Memorial Day weekend. We met Jim and his wife, Jennifer, in the courtroom. I wished the class good luck and thanked them again for choosing Flight 191 as their project.

I was on the verge of tears all day, especially as we waited for the presentations to get underway in the courtroom. Although the exact dates were different, May 28th versus May 25th, having this presentation take place on the Friday of Memorial Day weekend was significant since the plane crashed on the Friday of a Memorial Day weekend 31 years prior. I felt this was another divine sign. Maybe this project might just catch the attention of someone listening.

MELODY ◆ They wowed us all in the courtroom by doing a 120-second rap, passionately laying out what needed to be done and why it should be done for a Flight 191 Memorial. They had a background of pictures and slides. It was an awesome presentation. I left knowing they would win. And, again, I couldn't help but think maybe a push for a Flight 191 Memorial would be possible!

KIM ◆ At the end of their presentation, there was an electric energy in the room. Melody and I hugged Jim and Jen. I remember applauding and finally letting that tear drop (and a few more) with a standing ovation. I thought to myself, all of the spirits of Flight 191 are here. I imagined my parents and all the spirits of Flight 191 clapping, whistling, and watching from above. I had one of my Dad's bow ties and one of Mom's hankies in my pocket for a spiritual connection.

Although no winners were announced that day in the courtroom, I had a sense that 60 plus 6th graders had sparked the judges' interest. Some of the judges were connected to the flight or remembered where they were when news broke of the crash in 1979.

As the students came back for dismissal, there were lots of high fives. Both of their teachers received accolades.

There were no words to express my gratitude to those 6th graders other than saying thank you.

If my hunch was right, their enthusiasm, empathy, and drive might have inspired others to honor and remember those lost on May 25th, 1979. They did so much to bring our story into the light and honor a day in history that happened many years before any of them were even born!

The *STARS ALIGN*

KIM ◆ If Mel, Jim, and I could have paid for the entire class and their teachers to go to Disney World, we would have. If my memory serves me right, the three of us did treat the class to an ice cream treat the following Friday in their classroom on behalf of all the families who lost a loved one on the flight.

In addition to the sweet treat, we wrote them a letter that we hoped expressed our gratitude for all the hard work they put into the project and presentation. Having the privilege of watching their presentation, we all had the sense that maybe somewhere, someplace, at some time, there would finally be a place or a plaque to simply remember and never forget.

MELODY ◆ After the students won the competition, their project went on to the national competition. They were also starting to gain some influential support. I was told of various supporters from Kim. She noted the likes of U.S. Representative Jan Schakowsky's office and attorney Thomas Demetrio. Ironically, my husband and brother had gone to his law office back in 1979 to see if our family should proceed with litigation against American Airlines.

We decided, as a family, not to file a lawsuit. Personally, I thought filing a case would have us constantly focusing on the crash instead of moving forward with our lives. We'd always be focused on those final 31

June 14, 2010

Dear Decatur Classical 6ᵗʰ Graders,

We wish we had the time to write each and every one of you a note. Hopefully you will accept this letter as a token of our appreciation, along with a sweet treat! There are no words to express our deep gratitude to all of you, Mrs. Allegretti, and Mrs. Sharping for your diligence and hard work associated with AA Flight 191. We know because of your hard work, a memorial marker will become a reality! That reality was clear to all of us who were privileged to witness your amazing presentation at the Dirksen Federal Building on Friday, May 28, 2010. Our only wish was that more family members and those closely related to Flight 191 could have been there.

We have no doubt that each and every one of you will go on in life to make a difference and impact our society and world in a positive way, as you already have! On behalf of our parents, Corrinne and Bill Borchers, the crew and passengers aboard Flight 191 and on the ground, who lost their lives, we thank you! On behalf of all the families and friends of those who died and whose lives were changed forever, we thank you from the bottom of our hearts.

Please know that each and every one of you have touched our hearts and just as the crash of Flight 191 on May 25, 1979 connected us to 272 other families, we will always be connected to each of you for making sure that 273 people and Flight 191 will be remembered, not lost or forgotten!!

With heartfelt thanks and appreciation,

The Borchers Family

Melody Smith, Jim Borchers and Kim Jockl

seconds of Mom and Dad's lives instead of all the great memories before then. The lawsuit might be more detrimental to all of our healing. Also, the lawyers informed us that because of their ages and our ages, the money received would not be that much greater, if at all, after attorneys' fees, than the settlement offered, and we would possibly be in litigation for years. Bob being a lawyer and me being a paralegal, we both knew how litigation could drag on for years. We settled with the insurance company of American Airlines for $200,000 in 1980.

However, to this day, our brother regrets not filing a suit against American Airlines. But he went along with the rest of us.

Thomas Demetrio also was one of the judges at the students' presentation. He litigated various cases from this crash and took it upon himself to write letters to American Airlines and Boeing to support this memorial in some fashion. The students were also looking at various types of memorials. They were looking at multiple sites, including a tree on the school property.

We knew a memorial at the crash site would not be feasible for people to get onto the airport grounds. So, the Kennedy Toll Plaza overlooking the site was one of the sites we looked at, but the state said it was unsafe because it was a truck stop, along with all the toll booths' activity.

KIM ◆ The students continued their letter-writing campaign, especially to American Airlines, asking for financial support. Dave Davis, from U.S. Representative Schakowsky's office, was present for the students' presentation and requested an encore presentation for the Representative to hear and see herself. This happened on June 7, 2010, in the multi-purpose room of Decatur Classical School. Again, the students hit a grand slam! Representative Schakowsky told the students to keep writing and designing and felt it was a project that deserved her support.

A few days later, the students received a response to the many letters sent to American Airlines. As one can read below, American Airlines stated that it sounded like a wonderful project, but, as a company, they are choosing to move on from this tragedy, wishing these students the best of luck.

"We do appreciate your efforts and desire for a memorial to those who lost their lives in the accident. As an airline, we feel that the memory of those lost so long ago is best remembered in the hearts of those who were touched by the accident. That would include American Airlines and its employees as we lost many colleagues and customers that day. While we will always remember Flight 191, it is our desire to move on from that terrible day. We hope to have your understanding of our perspective.

To the sixth grade class, you are clearly part of an excellent learning environment at Decatur Classical. Thank you again for your letters, and have a wonderful summer break."

When the students shared the letter with me and Ms. Kukielka (the principal), I was not surprised, but I was still disappointed that this was the response given to a group of 6th graders asking American Airlines to finally do the right thing.

Ironically, the day American Airlines responded to the Decatur students, the law office of Corboy and Demetrio was writing a letter on behalf of the students to both American Airlines and the Boeing Company, who was also responsible for the crash of Flight 191.

After the students did their presentation for U.S. Representative Schakowsky, she told them to put together a design, projected cost, and possible locations so that when she met with them in a few weeks, they would all have a better idea of what they needed financially to make their project a reality. My husband Peter and I volunteered to take pictures for the students to include in their possible memorial locations when they met with Representative Schakowsky again.

At the end of June, the students met again with Representative Schakowsky. An actual dollar amount was discussed based on the students' research. After this meeting, American Airlines and Boeing received another letter from Schakowsky.

Even though the students were on summer break, and even though they were moving on to different schools, they continued to work feverishly all summer long — at home and often at the school. They were still making calls and hoped the Congresswoman backing their project might just be the key.

In addition to writing letters, the Congresswoman's office was also helping the students look for possible locations for the memorial. By the end of summer, Lake Park in Des Plaines became part of the conversation. This park was part of State Senator Dan Kotowski's district of representation.

The summer of 2010 continued to be wait and see. It was sometimes difficult to watch from a distance, not allowing myself to give an opinion or idea unless asked by the students to do so.

But then, one quiet August afternoon, while I was working on schedules and manning the office phones by myself, the phone rang. I answered in my standard, everyday way.

"Decatur Classical School, how may I help you? Mrs. Jockl speaking."

The caller asked to speak with one or both of the 6th-grade teachers in charge of the project, and I explained it was summer break, but I would be happy to take a message. The caller's message was that he was from American Airlines and they hoped to provide *some* financial support, but not what the students were requesting. American Airlines was supporting many other worthwhile causes at this time...

I cleared my throat and repeated my name.

"My name is Kim Jockl, the daughter of Corrine and Bill Borchers, who died on American Airlines Flight 191. I have not had a parent in my life for over 30 years. On behalf of my family and all the families who lost a loved one, your message is unacceptable."

I tried my best to keep professional, but I have no doubt the caller could hear the anger in my voice. He did offer his condolences but said again they would try to help the students in some way. I jotted down the message and phone number. Said goodbye, hung up the phone, and then I sat in the office and cried. I was shaking, I was upset, mad, and strangely, this was the first time I had actually "met" American Airlines. And they *still* would not try to make things right.

I passed the message along to the teachers, the principal, and U.S. Representative Schakowsky's office. I know many letters continued to be written. The Congresswoman was in contact with American Airlines and Boeing. By summer's end, the teachers received another call from American Airlines. American Airlines stated they would like to discuss with the students and teachers how they could honor the financial request! I set up the conference call for later that week.

After the conference call, American Airlines had committed to pay $20,000!

The 2010-2011 school year began with the excitement of a possible memorial and the challenge of transporting the students (who were now 7th graders) from their new schools to meet and continue to work on their project in our building. The current 6th graders would also support and continue the search for families of those lost on the flight, but keeping that original group together was essential and would be hard to pull off.

Both classes, the current 6th graders and the now 7th graders met with Janie Morrison, the District Director, and other representatives from State Senator Dan Kotowski's office to discuss and finalize the details of the memorial based on the students' design from last year. The cherry on top of all of this was attending the Constitutional Rights Foundation of Chicago's luncheon and conference to see Mrs. Allegretti and Mrs. Sharping awarded the Edward J. Lewis II Teachers of the Year Award. The project received national recognition, and the teachers accepted the Constitutional Rights Foundation Blue Ribbon of Superior award on behalf of the students.

What a week!

The next hurdle was securing the land in Lake Park.

MELODY ◆ Sometime in December of 2010, I was asked by students to attend a meeting with Senator Kotowski's office and teachers to hear about other possible memorial sites. The discussion focused on Lake Park in Des Plaines since it was close to the airport and offered a good location to gather. Plus, the former head of Parks and Recreation for the State of Illinois had resided in Des Plaines and also died on Flight 191. Janie mentioned NILCO, along with other companies, as possible contractors to build the memorial. When I heard NILCO, I said to Kim, "That's Dick Lamkey's company." Dick and his wife, Nita, were friends of Bob and mine from college, and they both knew our mom and dad. I couldn't help thinking this was a good sign for this location!

In December 2010, I saw Dick at a Christmas party and told him about the possible memorial at Lake Park and how his company was mentioned at the students' presentation. He said he wanted to be a part of this project if it went ahead at Lake Park. He talked about how much he liked Bill and Nudy and that Flight 191 needed a memorial.

What an incredible coincidence. Things continued to keep connecting together!

KIM ✦ With a financial commitment from American Airlines, plus having the politicians and the village of Des Plaines and their Park District involved, a very strong possibility of a memorial happening made the meeting on December 9th, 2010 very exciting. These students presented all their ideas, sketches, and shared all they had done with District Director Janie Morrison from Senator Kowtoski's Office. Janie would now be a critical liaison between the students, teachers, Des Plaines, and companies involved in the actual building of the project. Senator Kotowski's office was determined to bring the students' ideas to life by the 32nd anniversary of the crash. Holy Cow! Pinch me now!

We were all very hopeful that a check for $21,500 would be on its way to Decatur Classical so there would be funds to accomplish the project. Janie also reached out to Melody and me, inviting us to a meeting at her office on January 11, 2011. She wanted to learn about our American Airlines Flight 191 journey before the Decatur Classical School 6th grade project.

MELODY ✦ Janie was not from Chicago and, initially, was not sure the importance of this memorial or why there had never been a memorial done at the time of the accident. So, Kim and I educated her on our journey and how this "Project Citizen" school competition came about. We also talked about American's refusal to give us the manifest, how they didn't help us, or even attend the 25th Anniversary. We informed her that after many letters from students and representatives and lawyers and Decatur's principal, American finally committed to financially supporting this memorial.

This meeting helped Janie realize the magnitude and everything that had gone into our efforts over the last several years. Now she was fully committed to getting this done.

KIM ✦ The check from American Airlines was not in the mail immediately as everyone had hoped. In fact, many more letters were sent to American Airlines to nudge this along.

But finally, in March (six months after their initial commitment), American Airlines made good on its promise to the students and teachers. The check arrived, and now the project could really get underway.

I sent an email to American Airlines thanking them for the check and requesting the official manifest so those lost on the flight could be acknowledged and appropriately identified at the memorial site. Here we were approaching the 32nd anniversary, and the response we continued to receive was, "We'll see what we can do."

Everyone assumed, including American Airlines, that Melody and I had an official manifest, but we didn't. And record-keeping in 1979 was not perfect by a long shot.

So, the bad news: Because of the delay in monetary support, and the uncertainty of an official manifest, our target date of May 25, 2011 was not going to happen.

But the good news: On May 18, 2011, a *Journal and Topics* article confirmed the details of Des Plaines approving the project. The Memorial site would open later in the fall!

Then, on August 15, 2011, the Decatur teachers, principal, and I received an email from Janie Morrison, stating that she and her office had finally achieved the milestone of locating every single person lost on Flight 191! They had tons of help from a private detective and the Department of Vital Records for Cook County, in addition to her wonderful interns. She told us everyone is committed to this great project, from the landscaper to the Des Plaines Park President. A date can now be set for the groundbreaking, which will happen soon. The stars were all aligned! Janie asked us to look over the list of names that would be sent to the engraver early the following week. Thank God for all of their hard work finding the names because, to the best of my knowledge, my request for an official manifest was never honored by American Airlines.

It wasn't long after that when other major newspapers shared the plans for the memorial.

On September 18, 2011, I took the following picture, confirming that dreams do come true. I cried knowing our parents and all who perished would never be forgotten. What a picture. What a moment. What a day!

Not long after this photo was taken, the memorial's construction began. Besides a memorial being built, Decatur School was busy calling, emailing, and searching for people connected to the flight to attend the

dedication. We kept a notebook in the school's main office as people from all over the country called to RSVP or simply called to tell the 6th graders thank you. Hundreds of emails to the teachers, students, and school re-iterated the same response over and over again: *I will be there. If I can't be there, I will be there in spirit.*

Everything was a team effort leading up to the event. Margo, the school secretary, helped in the ordering of the hundreds of ribbons to be distributed at the dedication. A Decatur parent in the printing industry took the program created by the students and printed it for free. Danny Wallen-berg directed the Decatur Classical Chicago Children's Choir every Friday during recess. The students rehearsed their songs, and I remember eating my lunch, crying in the office listening to them. Tears, laughter, and every emotion in between filled the school, in addition to just plain excitement.

On Wednesday or Thursday before the Dedication, Marianne, Sue, and I met a reporter from the Daily Herald out at the wall to be interviewed. This wall would allow others to do the same: gather, remember, and never forget. Pretty sure I cried the entire way home that night. Seeing all those bricks and all those names so beautifully displayed, the reality sank in: these were all the 273 people who died in the same place, in the same way, in a field, just down the road in a fiery crash on what was otherwise a beautiful, sunny day in May. It was incredibly emotional. For the first time, I wasn't afraid to look. I felt the spirits of Flight 191 were finally at peace, Mom and Dad included.

The stage was set: the programs in bundles, the ribbons in baskets, the paper and crayons to do a rubbing of your loved one's brick were ready and waiting. Speeches were written, and all that was left to handle was something we had no control over... the weather.

But I knew, in my heart, the spirits of Flight 191 would help us out in that department too.

Photo courtesy of Lisa Haring

MIRACLES *do* HAPPEN

MELODY ◆ While driving to the memorial dedication, I reflected on how we arrived at this triumphant day. It was truly a miracle! I felt a great sense of gratitude to the various people who helped me on this journey.

Certainly, my husband, Bob. He was there for me when the plane crashed and every day after through the years of my grieving. He supported my family and me emotionally, and he knew how important this memorial was for the three of us. I'm grateful for my children, Chris and Jordan. Chris, being the only one alive at the time of the crash, I hope he doesn't remember those endless days, months, and years of tears. Fast forward to the present, and here they are bringing their babies — my grandchildren — to the memorial to honor their great grandparents, who they've only seen in photos and heard about in the retelling of family stories.

And how fitting that my friends Nita and Dick were part of our story with Dick's company building this memorial wall that we'd gather around today. Many other friends and neighbors would be there who never met Mom and Dad but felt they knew them through my stories.

KIM ◆ As I drove by myself down Touhy Avenue on that sunny Saturday, I remember having a conversation out loud with Mom and Dad. I talked to them about life, the day ahead, and the 32 years without them. I was trying my best not to cry so as not to mess up my makeup. I wanted to look my

best for such a big Red Letter Day!

I passed the CPD Canine Dog Training Facility on Touhy and thought back to when Melody, Jim, and I began our journey, looking and searching for the actual crash site. I felt terrible that Michael Lux, the son of Flight 191's Captain, Walter Lux, would not be with us today to see a dream we shared come to fruition. We'd learned of his passing when the students tried reaching out to him at the start of their project. Melody and I felt horrible learning his life was cut short by cancer. Leading up to this day, I cried many tears sharing and engaging in email and phone conversations with many family members who reached out to Decatur Classical regarding the Dedication. I was anxious to meet many of those whom I'd gotten to know via those communications.

I was excited to share this day, not only with my immediate family but also with our extended family and many friends who knew "Nudy and Bill." Everyone who was part of my journey in 1979 would witness, 32 years later, that miracles do happen.

I wrapped up my conversation with Mom and Dad. I thanked them for guiding me. I told them I knew they were always with me — on the good days, the bad days, and all the in-between days. Not only did I survive those bad years following the crash, but I went on to have a beautiful family of my own, a strong teaching career, and became an administrator at one of the top schools in the state. I wish I could've shared those experiences with Mom and Dad, but I know they've been with me in spirit.

As I turned the corner to park in the Abbott Labs parking lot across from the park, I was overwhelmed to see so many news and media trucks lined up on Miner Street next to the park. I started to gather things from my car. I had buttons created with Mom and Dad's photo on them. The photo was from the same wedding where the cover photo of this book was taken; a celebration one week before the crash. I'd distribute the buttons to all of our connections at the event.

In addition to the buttons, I took some of Mom's hankies, had them dry-cleaned and pressed, and gave one to Sue, Beth, Marianne, and others to have a tangible connection between them and Mom. I took one of Dad's bow ties and made sure to have it with me.

To this day, whether it's a wedding, funeral, or a family Red Letter Day, I tuck one of Mom's hankies and Dad's bow ties into my pocket or purse to symbolize their presence and spiritual connection.

Alright. One last run-through of the checklist.

Buttons. Check.

Ribbons. Check.

Programs and booklets. Check.

Hankey and bow tie. Check.

Ready. Set.

Go!

Mom, Dad, and all who were lost on Flight 191, today is your day. Finally, a place where all of your names are displayed, together, for all to remember!

The stage and chairs were set, and the spirits of Flight 191 took care of the weather (as we knew in our hearts they would). No rain! Sunny, but very windy. Sue and I arrived early. Sue had the idea to put some of the blue ribbons out in the tree behind the Memorial wall. The wind was swirling and increasing throughout the morning. It was as if the spirits of Flight 191 were gathering with us, letting their presence be known. The flickering ribbons really brought that thought to life.

MELODY ♦ This was my first time at Lake Park in Des Plaines. I was blown away by the location, and I couldn't believe the size of the crowd. There were hundreds of people. This was a far cry from the 15 families gathered on the 25th!

The program was colorful, musical, and meaningful. Seeing the wall with the 273 names, it really hit me that now, at last, they all had a final resting place together. People went up to the wall and traced the names of loved ones. In the ensuing years, this would become a favorite activity of my grandchildren whenever we would visit the memorial.

The numerous people I met from other Flight 191 families was a bit overwhelming. Many of these families' emotions were still raw as if the

273 Lost, 191 Forgotten

The Journey of the Students of Decatur Classical School

Our journey began about 730 days ago as we sat in our classroom, at Decatur Classical School, brainstorming topics for Project Citizen. Project Citizen, a national civic education program for 5th – 8th grade students coordinated in Illinois by the Constitutional Rights Foundation of Chicago, gave us the opportunity to look at issues in our community, analyze policies and try to make a difference. Timing is everything in this world. Mrs. Jockl, our assistant principal, walked into our discussion and with our teachers' prompting, told us the moving story of how her life dramatically changed on May 25th, 1979. Her story of the 273 lost and Flight 191 forgotten deeply moved each and every one of us and we all knew then and there we needed to try and make a difference.

In the months to come, we dove into endless research trying to understand the tragic and historic events of Flight 191. We discovered that this was the single worst air crash outside a terrorist attack, yet never recognized. With each piece of evidence and sad, personal story uncovered, we appreciated the depth of this tragedy and the importance to establish a memorial. Most of all, we learned that the Flight 191 tragedy not only affected the families, friends and colleagues who lost loved ones, but also the first responders, recovery teams and community members who played important roles in the aftermath. Additionally, it has affected all individuals who travel by air today, due to changes in safety and airplane maintenance procedures. We realized that memorializing such tragedies is necessary in the grieving process, and came to understand that when someone you love becomes a memory, that memory is a treasure.

In May of 2010, we presented our findings to a prestigious panel of experts that included Dave Davis from the office of Congresswoman Schakowsky, Thomas Demetrio from the law offices of Demetrio and Corboy, Teri Brady from The Federal Aviation Administration and Ted Gibbs from the office of Governor Quinn at the Dirksen Federal Building. These individuals were moved by the story we told, your story. Charged by Thomas Demetrio, of Demetrio and Corboy, we designed a memorial themed with the concepts of nature and healing.   Our project and your story gained local, state and national recognition. We continued our journey and met with Congresswoman Jan Schakowsky during the summer of 2010. Congresswoman Schakowsky was deeply moved by this story, realizing the need for this memorial and became a champion of our cause. She enlisted Senator Dan Kotowski and after several months, this beautiful location in the Des Plaines community was chosen. Nilco Landscape Solutions helped make our vision actually materialize and so today, we dedicate this meaningful and beautiful memorial.

Our involvement with Project Citizen and establishing this memorial taught us many things. We discovered that you are never too young to start making a positive impact on society and change is often the result of hard work and dedication. We realized that, "No--can't--won't--and too difficult" are not options when a wrong needs to be made right. As future leaders, we have learned the importance of listening to children for often they have important messages to share and hope to carry that notion into our adulthood. We sincerely thank the adults who took us seriously and rallied behind our cause. You have empowered us by taking the time to be our audience and supporters and gave us the sense that we can make a difference in this world. We have realized the importance of telling our loved ones how much they mean to us, for everything can change in a single moment. Establishing this memorial has given us critical life lessons.

Inspired by the words, "They deserve, we deserve, history deserves a memorial, today, October 15, 2011, the Decatur Classical Class of 2010 can respectfully say, "We Remember Them."

For information regarding contributions for upkeep and ongoing enhancements of the Flight 191 Memorial, please contact Des Plaines Park District, Gene Haring, 847-391-5087 or gene.haring@DPParks.org

To stay connected with individuals associated with AA Flight 191 and the Memorial, please visit: flight191.org or contact Andrew Cook at 224-999-0001.

crash had just happened. They were still hurting, yet they were so thankful to talk to someone like them and have a physical place to visit.

KIM ♦ So often, the key players in making a dream a reality do not see their hard work pay off. We were all blessed to be there! There was so much love and respect filling the audience. Once again, we were blessed to have

Father Michael Zaniolo (Father Mike), who accompanied us out to the crash site the first time, continue in his role of prayer, comforter, and spiritual leader. He blessed the memorial and sprinkled the Memorial space with sod from the actual crash site.

The thunder of clapping and the sounds of the billowing gusting winds were mighty and emotional.

MELODY ⬦ Another key connector for me was Gail Dunham, who started the National Air Disaster Alliance, and she would be there today from the East Coast. She'd been a stewardess and saw after crashes that people needed assistance from the airlines beyond just medical help. She was the person who encouraged me to contact American Airlines to get them involved and shed light on what was now being done for families after air disasters. She kept giving me ideas and encouragement to get a memorial accomplished but said we would need a manifest from American to reach more people and she would see if her contacts could help. At the 25th she sent representatives from her organization but for this dedication she was attending in person!

Our family in 2011 at the Dedication looked much different than our family grouping in 1979. Spouses, grandchildren, and in-laws were now wonderful additions, of whom we love, but will always be sad that most never got to meet our Mom and Dad. We are all thankful for the close-knit family that we have.

JIM ◆ With the anniversary date always right there with Memorial Day weekend, I can't help but think about all those backyard BBQs on California Avenue.

What I would give to watch just one more time, Dad, much to Mom's dismay, douse the charcoal briquettes with gasoline and then from ten feet away (out of necessity), strike and throw a match at the grill. We'd all witness the ignition and ensuing fireball rivaling a Hollywood pyrotechnic stunt! It's a memory in time that came and went in an instant, but it's one I will forever cherish. Just one of hundreds.

What I failed to realize at the time was how the love and diligence of my parents would later in life serve me to survive the inevitable and unforeseen negative events which we all must deal with eventually.

November 2, 2011

Dear Decatur Class of 2010,

Proud, grateful, touched, poised and moved are some of the words that come to mind when I think of all of you and reflect on the incredible Project Citizen journey you took us on, along with your teachers, Mrs. Allegretti and Mrs. Sharping! For us as a family, this journey began with all of you at the Dirksen Federal Building on May 25, 2010; ironically, on the 31st anniversary of the crash. Melody, Jim and I had the privilege of witnessing your "273 Lost; 191 Forgotten" presentation and we knew it was one special project, as it brought tears to our eyes and clearly moved every person in that courtroom. For us as a family, your presentation on that day would have been enough, as it was the first time anyone had publicly argued the need for a permanent memorial or marker of AA Flight 191. Never in our wildest dreams did we think that your hard work leading up to that day would result in "273 Lost; 191 **Remembered**" on October 15, 2011 with over 1000 people in attendance at Lake Park to listen to your journey and share in the dedication of a beautiful, fitting memorial for those who lost their lives.

We want you to know how thankful we are to each and every one of you and how proud you should be of your accomplishment! Your project that began in the halls of Decatur spread and touched thousands of individuals and made a difference in all of our lives. We now have a place, as do all who are connected to this flight, to not only remember our parents, but all of the people who lost their lives together on May 25, 1979. For us, seeing all of the names together, in such a beautiful setting, brought a sense of peace and comfort to us and hopefully to all of them. When you began to read the names at the dedication, the wind seemed to almost stop. We can only imagine that the spirits of Flight 191 were sitting on a cloud looking down and saying…"Shhh…the students are reading our names and listen….They Remembered! Flight 191 was not forgotten!"

All of you and your teachers will always have a special place in our hearts for making that wildest dream a reality! Our hopes and dreams for all of you is that you continue to impact the world and make a difference in people's lives. We have no doubt that you will.

Bravo, High Fives, and Heartfelt Thanks to ALL of You,
The Family of Corrinne and Bill Borchers (Nudy and Bill)…
…Mrs. Jockl, Melody Smith and Jim Borchers

We were so very fortunate to have Nudy and Bill for what now seems to be a painfully short period of time. My advice and our purpose in writing this book is to tell our family (and all readers) to grab, savor, and enjoy every second you can with your siblings and parents, because as each second occurs, it is past. The repetition of these traditions and moments will serve you well in the future.

MELODY ◆ I, along with every other family member, could not thank these students enough for what they had accomplished. It certainly was one of those Red Letter Days for our family that will be etched in our hearts forever.

The letter from State Senator Kotowski summed up everyone's feelings of having been part of such a special project and a much overdue memorial.

The memorial gave us a place to call home. One beautiful, meaningful spot to rally around.

A PLACE *to* GATHER

MELODY ◆ 2019 marked a very significant year. This would be the 40th anniversary of Flight 191.

But I was filled with reservations. We had so many other major family happenings this year I didn't know if we could also plan something big for the 40th.

Our list included:

• My nephew Matthew's wedding in May
• My brother-in-law Peter's retirement
• My youngest granddaughter Kinsley's First Holy Communion
• Me and Bob's 50th wedding anniversary in August
• Jim's 70th birthday in the fall.

However, after meeting people at the wall on the 39th Anniversary, Kim and I knew we needed to initiate and orchestrate the 40th Anniversary for more than just our family. It also became clear to both of us we needed to reach out to the first and second responders from the day of the crash.

KIM ◆ Early in the year, our family was gathered to celebrate my son Matthew and his fiancé Sheri's engagement. The two stood up to make an announcement.

Matthew and Sheri found a venue for their wedding, and now they could finally lock in a date.

Their date of choice: May 25th, 2019.

My heart sank. But I lifted a glass to toast their happiness. When I got home, I texted them and asked if they could change their first choice of wedding date. I told them they probably didn't realize this, but it was the anniversary of Flight 191, a big one, one that ends in a zero, 40 years. We would be doing something special to remember Mom and Dad. I also told them I didn't want to share May 25th with another significant family event, if possible. They immediately responded and changed the date to May 11th, for which I was very grateful.

To say our party/event plates were full for 2019 was an understatement. With all of these happenings coming up, Melody and I started to think the best option would be simply acknowledging May 25th with our family, something low-key. Low stress.

But that all changed when we went to the Memorial wall on May 25, 2018. We ran into Ron Walerowicz, FAA Fuel Safety Inspector/ARFF Training Instructor at the Chicago Fire Department. In his role at O'Hare, Flight 191 is mentioned in all of his trainings.

He and others we crossed paths with at the Memorial Wall that day asked what was happening for the 40th anniversary. With all of these inquiries, we knew we needed to set the wheels in motion for a memorial service, especially since it was the first big anniversary — one that ended in a zero — where there was actually a place to gather.

So, on June 7th of 2018, we called Gene Haring at the Des Plaines Park District and asked if we could plan something for May 25th. We asked if he and his staff would like to join our grand committee of two.

MELODY ◆ In September of 2018, our next planning journey began. We were joined by Ron Walerowicz from the Chicago Fire Department, Gene Haring and Brian Panek from the Des Plaines Park District, and representatives from the City of Des Plaines. As the months went on, we acquired additional members like Leo Karrall, who'd been with us on the crash site prior to the 25th. He was one of the people responsible for helping us commemorate the 25th Anniversary at O'Hare.

The planning for the 40th Anniversary was totally different from our 25th-anniversary experience. We had a group of extremely capable people helping us make this event happen. End of September 2018, we had an incredible first meeting where we talked about logistics, publicity, who to invite, who to read off names, and how to utilize a Facebook group. It was incredible. I'd say we'd come a long way since that very first internet search nearly two decades earlier!

KIM • The major difference between planning this gathering and the 25th is we had social media, the Facebook group dedicated to Flight 191, and Des Plaines to contact the media and papers. Having the Facebook group made it much easier to spread the word. We also had people in place to connect with who we did not have at the 25th Anniversary.

As always, Todd from Journal and Topics was willing to help get the word out regarding the upcoming event. I also connected and shared details with numerous fire departments through a friend whose path I crossed at Triton College and who was involved in their first responder training program. She did a small presentation to fire department representatives from numerous municipalities who remembered the crash and knew colleagues who actually responded to the crash.

MELODY • In reaching out to various first and second responders associated with the crash, we realized how right our instinct was to bring them into our group. Many of these firemen, policemen, and state troopers were still experiencing the effects of this crash personally, 40 years later. Some would commit to participating at the 40th event but then renege due to anxieties, not wanting to recall this event, and generally feeling a malaise when thinking about their involvement with this crash.

Throughout those hectic months leading up to the 40th, Kim and I talked to many more people who witnessed the crash and its immediate aftermath. I think it was the first time we realized that all we went through as a family in our loss, in many ways, could not compare to what these individuals experienced and how that day impacted their lives, forever, in a negative way. Over the years, we've been able to focus on the good memories with Mom and Dad instead of just their deaths. From our conversations, we learned this wasn't always the case with others impacted. Cliché phrases like, "Just give it time," or, "Time heals all wounds," life is rarely that simple. While visiting the memorial on the 39th Anniversary, we met a State Trooper paying his respects with his wife. The former state trooper kept apologizing for not being able to help or save anyone immediately following the crash. The first responder explained how they couldn't get to the victims who were so far down in the ground due to the impact of the plane crashing. This was something we had never heard before and was a new visual to put in our heads of the actual crash site. We reached out to him to be a reader at the 40th Anniversary, but he could not commit.

The grief experienced from Flight 191 can take a whole lifetime to work through. Our only hope is that through these anniversary memorials, through the group we've created, and now, even through this book, we might help this First Responder and many more people reach the sense of healing and closure our family has experienced over the years.

KIM ✦ Every Thursday, starting four years ago, we met for "book club" at my house. This was another new journey for us, turning these stories and years of information into a book. We'd go through Flight 191 memorabilia and papers and begin writing chapters. But there was also lots of talk of something for the wedding, Bob and Melody's 50th, or Pete's retirement. The 40th Anniversary of Flight 191 was mixed in with everything else going on in our family.

Time kept flying by with an event every month. In March, we hosted the bridal shower. In April, there was a bachelor party and a retirement party. Kinsley's Communion kicked things off in May, followed by a rehearsal dinner and wedding on May 11th. Whew!

After the wedding, we only had one solid week to finalize the plans for the 40th. We met with the committee for the final time on May 22nd to finish the day's event.

MELODY ✦ This time around, we had the luxury of being contacted by the media through Des Plaines media outreach efforts. It was not a battle to get the word out. Kim also reached out to the reporter Vince Gerasole since his interview with us on the 30th Anniversary was a catalyst to the memorial wall being built. He was a significant part of our journey, and we wanted to bring him into this next milestone. Our family and other families associated with this crash were interviewed by TV, newspapers, and magazines. Our family's interviews on TV also included our brother. He wanted to be more a part of this process and express his feelings more publicly than he had done in the past.

However, for all three of us, reliving this event, even 40 years later, it still brought tears to our eyes, no matter how many times we told our story.

KIM ◆ In addition to many stories and interviews shared on TV and in the newspapers, I was also in contact with Kori Finley from the Chicago Tribune who was working on developing projects that would allow for families of victims of the crash to post pictures and give a face to those lost and tell who they were. This was never done before, and I was more than happy to help Kori by posting details in the Friends and Family Flight 191 Facebook group. Many did post pictures, and many of those individual stories were available to read online and in print.

The photos gave a face to many of those names and reading stories about who they were brought their spirits to life. Kori's project and all the journalists involved really did a great job telling the story of Flight 191 in print and online. What's wonderful about the online version is how it's a living document people can readily access and add to the many stories and pictures of those lost.

Like Melody said, telling our story was still emotional, and so was seeing these stories in print and online. Unfortunately, there was also a story about the possibility of a road being built on the crash site where everyone perished. We were grateful this story did not overshadow the 40th-anniversary remembrance!

MELODY ◆ Driving to the 40th Anniversary, I heard a news story on the radio about the sale of the Flight 191 crash site to developers to build an additional roadway to the airport. I was so thankful to have this permanent memorial at Lake Park so I didn't have to worry about the actual crash site anymore, or what commercial projects would be developed there. I still hope, in the future, there will at least be some sign noting the loss of 273 lives on that site. But again, the memorial site gives us a home base and fills me with a sense of peace and closure.

Oh, one more thing tied to O'Hare. In the fall of 2018, the three of us saw pictures of the runway (32R) being permanently closed at O'Hare. This is the runway Flight 191 took off at.

As I pulled up to the parking lot, I saw Bev Ottaviano, my co-worker for many years at the Arlington Heights Historical Society, attending this event with her husband. She quickly offered to hand out programs and do whatever was needed. She'd heard all my stories while planning the 25th Anniversary. She also taught one of the children of a crash victim. She was their teacher the day their father died. She reconnected with that student by chance at the 40th memorial and met her children. What a small world!

It was a sunny, but again an extremely windy day, just like we'd experienced at the dedication. My sister and I always talked about the wind and how all the spirits must have been awakened at these large gatherings. It also rained for a few days before the event, so the area was very muddy, and there was concern about setting up the hundreds of chairs. But the grounds crew, led by Brian Panek, did a remarkable job prepping the area.

KIM ◆ Although I have no scientific evidence to support my theory, I like to think the wind is all the spirits of Flight 191 gathering and letting us know they are with us and are pleased we've never forgotten them.

Once again, as I did at the dedication, I had a conversation with Mom and Dad as I drove down Touhy Avenue.

I told them — especially Mom — that although it took us 23 years to embrace her message that something had to be done, today we made good on all her heartfelt spiritual messages. I gave her and Dad a brief update on where we all were as a family, and I hoped they would be proud, especially of the three of us. I hoped that they were not only with us in spirit today but had been, and would be, shining down on all of us and the Red Letter Days this year.

As I pulled into the lot at Abbott and walked across the street to the park, I was overwhelmed by the number of first responders dressed in full uniform, the number of people already there, and the many friends and family who took the time to share in this beautiful 40th remembrance ceremony.

The program began on time under the direction and support of Gene Haring and the Des Plaines team, as well as Ron and the Chicago Fire Department, and Father Mike. Gene welcomed the crowd and all the readers of names (representing groups connected to Flight 191).

As we took our seats, Melody and I turned to each other and gave each other a high five. Totally spontaneous moment. But with Jim sitting in front of us as a reader of names, our entire family gathered in various locations, and even though it was tons of work organizing and planning amidst a very busy 2019, I am so glad we listened to our hearts and helped make it happen.

After the Color Guard and welcome by Gene and recognition of special guests, Melody and I kicked off the program with the story of our

Flight 191 journey. Not an easy task for us to succinctly tell in two minutes, and trust me, there were many edits and rewrites involved!

We've included our full speeches in the back of this book but for now, I just wanted to share my closing paragraph.

> *"We don't meet people by accident. They're meant to cross our path for a reason. The blessing of this journey, for us, is all the wonderful people we've met and stories shared since 2002...bringing us to today...this First Anniversary that ends in a Zero of which there is a place to gather, remember, and never forget American Airlines Flight 191."*

The Ringing of the Bell and Reading of the Names

At exactly 3:04, we all stood and turned toward the direction of the crash. At the same time, 31 bells tolled, signifying the number of seconds American Airlines Flight 191 was in the air.

Names of Readers who read aloud the names of those lost on Flight 191

Ed Mac McCall (Chief of Operations at O'Hare at time of the crash)

John Kenney (Forensic Dentist on Site)

Jim Borchers (Lost both parents)

Ryan Wangman (Decatur Classical Student part of the Flight 191 Memorial Project)

Gene Haring (Des Plaines Park District)

Adam Wesolowski-Mantilla (Decatur Classical Student part of the Flight 191 Memorial Project)

Saniya Merchant (Decatur Classical Student part of the Flight 191 Memorial Project)

Lina Kapp (Decatur Classical Student part of the Flight 191 Memorial Project)

Bill Hart (Lost his Dad)

Dick Lamkey (Built Memorial based on Student's design)

Bryson Lang/Joy Lang (Lost both parents)

Bill Klan (First Responder)

Beth Allegretti/Marianne Sharping (Teachers who led CRF Project with students at Decatur Classical School)

Sue Kukielka (Principal of Decatur Classical School at time of Memorial Project and Dedication)

Gary Schwartz (Lost both parents)

Tim Sampey (CFD)

Charles Roy (CFD)

Leo Karrall (O'Hare official)

MELODY • It was enlightening to meet many of the readers of names that day. Some I knew, but many I had only talked to through emails. I learned of their expertise and how much they had endured through the whole identification process, which lasted for many weeks and months.

On the identification side of things, one of the stories Kim and I heard came from a local man who lost his wife in the crash. She was never identified by her remains, along with about 30 other people who were never physically identified in this crash. Turns out, our mom had been in the last group of physically identified. He told us he was contacted by American Airlines. They flew him out to California where a casket for his wife and about 30 other caskets were laid to rest. After the burial, he was flown back to Illinois. How crazy was that! We also heard of a married couple who perished on the flight but only one was physically identified, and the other was buried out in California with the other people not physically identified. I realized, again, how fortunate our family was to have both Mom and Dad identified and buried here. Others were not so lucky!

Despite the wind, the water salute went off beautifully to end the program. Not only did Ron recognize all the First Responders, but he also explained the significance of the ceremonial water salute and its symbolism.

"We conclude today's 40th Anniversary with a Water Salute over the Memorial Site," Ron announced to the crowd. "Today's Water Salute will be four 10-second bursts of water over the Memorial Site to commemorate the four decades that have passed since 25 May 1979. In closing, I'd like to read the words on the dedication plaque:

'We remember Flight 191. Let us not forget the victims of May 25, 1979, who helped assure the safety of all who have boarded an airliner since that tragic event. When someone you love becomes a memory, the memory becomes a treasure.'

We had a chance to honor all of the heroes from that day in what was an incredibly emotional moment.

At this time we ask that all Fire, Police, Paramedics, First Responders, 2nd responders, and those who ran towards the crash site to help those lost and injured and those responders who stayed for weeks to help in the recovery and ID process of our loved ones or those whose relatives were first responders in 1979 and are here today, please stand up so we can respectfully recognize you. Our deepest heartfelt thanks!"

We thanked Ron for organizing this tribute from the Fire Department and were thankful the water salute became part of the program.

Once again, Father Mike scattered sod from the crash site and sprinkled Holy Water along the Memorial to connect the crash site with the Memorial down Touhy Avenue.

Father Mike's Dedication and Blessing was very special as he continues to be our spiritual leader of Flight 191 from our initial visit to the site, to the 25th Anniversary, to masses at O'Hare, to the Dedication of the Memorial, and once again at the 40th Anniversary.

After meeting so many families that day, we now hoped they had a clearer picture of how two sisters' journey brought us all together.

After the ceremony, the Smith-Borchers-Jockl families headed to the Smith house and invited all our friends and family in attendance back to eat and drink. What a memorable Red Letter Day for our family!

The day ended with sharing a Moscow Mule or two and a buffet of food in honor of Mom and Dad and Memorial Days past. We laughed and shared stories with people who knew Mom and Dad and others who knew them through us along with all of our family.

Our initial motivations on this journey where we finally "went there," opening up the file cabinet, was to find where our parents died, recognize, and remember Flight 191. Our journey ended 17 years later on the 40th Anniversary at a permanent memorial in Lake Park. This unbelievable and winding journey led us to meet so many wonderful people and experience and share in the tears and laughter of many who share the loss of a loved one or who are connected in some way to both Flight 191 and us. We will be forever grateful to all the significant people we spoke of for making Lake Park a reality. We really thought someday we'd simply find a place to hang a plaque with all of the names lost on May 25, 1979. Never in our wildest dreams did we imagine a gathering like this, in a setting like this, with a Memorial like this! How blessed we are in spite of this tragedy!

JIM ◆ While sitting with the readers, who were all connected to the flight in some way, two small world connections come to mind.

As a rule, I would always avoid discussions or questions about Flight 191 at work. It just didn't seem appropriate. Even insensitive. In retrospect, one conversation I wish I would have pursued was with Ed McCall who was Chief of Operations at O'Hare Field at the time of the crash. We knew each other through the bar business. Ed offered to help answer any questions I might have concerning the crash. At the time I think I didn't want to impose on a friend. I wish I would have. Ed kindly returned to Chicago to be a fellow reader of victims' names at the 40th memorial.

Another remembrance involved a fellow bar owner who was also a suburban firefighter. We had known each other for years, and our discussions would typically be late at night over beers. Mostly about our shared crazy experiences in the hospitality industry. On one of these occasions, though, out of the blue, he informed me that his fire company was the first truck on the scene at the crash site. He didn't want to discuss it, he just wanted to express his condolences and that when he retired he wanted me to have his helmet. That was it. Nothing more said. A couple of years later, upon his retirement, he did just that. When I called to ask him if he might be interested in being a name reader at the 40th anniversary, he adamantly refused in a manner that signaled there would be no more conversation about it. I gathered it was just too painful to revisit.

KIM • There are so many moments to reflect upon experiencing this 40th memorial. There isn't enough time to engage in long conversations at gatherings like this. What I carry with me and cherish from this day are the strong embraces from so many, as they introduced themselves as the sister, the brother, the husband, or the wife of someone our parents died with. It's a feeling and connection, as brief as it is, that sticks with you. Strangers with whom we share a life-changing and traumatic event. Some have overcome it, and others not yet.

Of course, sharing it with my family, friends, and colleagues from different ages and paths in my life was very special. Same with sharing it with friends and family who knew Mom and Dad, who lived that horrible day with us. Sharing it with friends and colleagues who remember the crash but never knew Mom and Dad is also special, as their support and crossing their path have made a difference in my life. Sharing this with the 6th graders who are now adults and in college, as well as their teachers, completed the journey for me. By participating in this celebration and remembrance of those lost, I hope they realize what a difference their school project made in all of our lives. Because of them, there is a place to gather, and the circle of those connected to Flight 191 continues to grow and heal. I only wish the whole group of 6th graders could have attended. Well, maybe that will be the goal for the 50th!

For all the bad days, there were many good days, the up days, and the down days. The book club days and, of course, all the Red Letter Days. I feel so blessed to share every step of this Flight 191 story and journey with Melody and Jim. We have been very fortunate to have each other to always lean on and count on.

I was quoted in an interview in the Tribune prior to the 40th that, "Joyous occasions and tragedies connect people. I'm hoping the 40th will be a joyous occasion so we can honor everyone who was connected with American Airlines Flight 191."

It certainly was a wonderful day and was so much more than we ever imagined. Finally, we have a place to gather, connect, honor, and remember all that is Flight 191.

The *GRAND* REVEAL

MELODY ◆ As Kim and I have always said, "There are two things that have defined our lives: standing on our heads and Flight 191."

This is our last chapter telling our journey with Flight 191, yet it's not. Flight 191 will forevermore be a part of our family's DNA, as long as Jim, Kim, and I are alive. And, hopefully, long after!

Many years ago, I was asked by a writer from Canada to describe both myself and my family after such a tragedy. This was 26 years after the fact, and I told him how I feel my brother, sister, and I care deeply about expressing our feelings to one another and the importance of our family and its history; something I'm not sure would have been as strong and ardent if Mom and Dad had lived longer in our midst.

Would we have been so conscious and committed to reflecting on our times spent together? Maybe. Maybe not. I've told my children the importance of developing their adult relationships with each other and their families without me and their dad always being there. Even though I always want to be part of their gatherings, it's okay for them to do things independently without us. Sometimes moms and dads get in the way. And I know there will come a time when we will no longer be there, and their strong sibling ties will keep them together to continue celebrating Red Letter Days.

It's also the importance my brother, sister, and I place on things from our past that has nothing to do with the item's value but rather the association with the item and the memories it triggers. The three of us have held onto things to forever make Mom and Dad part of our existing lives. Many years later, we're sometimes able to say it should go, or we'll lament about the items we didn't take when our family's home was robbed and sold. I had to explain this all to my now-grown children when I started showing up at their houses with things that I'd saved of theirs and how they needed to make the decision to hold on or pitch it.

One time Camy and Elle, my granddaughters, had an assignment to ask their grandma what she was like in first grade. By coincidence, I actually saved a letter from first grade answering the question, "What do you want to be when you grow up?" I had written this to my parents with a photo of me and how I wanted to be either a ballet dancer or a nun. It was just perfect that I still had this letter!

So, to me, why I hold onto things is to hold on to that period in time and the memories that go with it. Those memories keep the stories alive.

Our story and the stories from those we've met over the years connected to Flight 191 are definitely unique. Very few people experience this type of unexpected tragedy, one that's played out on the national news. But everyone experiences the death of a loved one at some point in their life, and each death has its particular issues to deal with. Having loved ones die suddenly is a jolt to everyone, but having no remains leaves one empty. I sometimes think if American Airlines had done the right thing, Flight 191 would still be part of my DNA, but the journey would have been very different.

I feel particularly strongly about the impact of sudden death on young adults. A few times in my adult life, I have reached out to young people under similar sudden loss of loved ones, knowing their need for support and understanding is greatly needed at that time. People always think of the youngest children, but the young children are cared for by others. It's the late teen and early 20s individuals who lose their anchor and are cast adrift. People think they will be fine, but as I saw, especially with my sister — a confident, self-assured, and intelligent individual — she was lost for a while. It wasn't until she got her footing back and was willing to accept help from her family and friends that her life got back on track. Even as a thirty-something mom and wife, I was also lost for a time. Fortunately, I had the support of my husband, family, and close friends that allowed me to ebb and flow through all the stages of sudden death and loss. Sometimes I was wild and crazy, and other times I was in a puddle of tears.

I am one of the lucky ones, along with my family, who made it through this with even stronger family ties and even deeper importance placed on family. When Mom wrote me that birthday letter over 40 years ago, she left me with the importance of family and passing this love on to my children and grandchildren. The Borchers-Smith-Jockl families are indeed blessed!

JIM • For the last four years, I have been continuously amazed at my sisters' ability to recall and document the events of the last 40+ years. Their recollections have helped me realize how much of that time I forgot or simply blocked from my memory.

Being in the middle between two sisters has had its challenges. They have more to say than I do. But I've loved these last four years of "Book Club" with both of them, and I think Thursdays have been very therapeutic for me. I have always gone along with their ideas — some crazier than others — but knew their hearts were in the right place, and they always assured me Mom was directing them, so I had to go along.

Looking back on things, I can see how after the crash I continued to show up and participate in family gatherings but I really don't have a clear memory of what took place and transpired for many years after Mom and Dad's death. Melody found an email I sent to her back in 2000 reflecting how much I still missed Mom and Dad and the void they left in my life, 20 years after the crash. Reading an email like that now, 20 some years later, I know I am in a better place and have accepted a life without Mom and Dad, all while still missing them.

These Thursday book clubs have allowed me to revisit a painful time and given me a willingness to express my feelings and loss. We all have a role to play, and mine is the silent supportive brother. However, at the 40th anniversary, I wanted to participate in the interviews and program and share my story with others for the first time. This is something Melody and Kim have been doing publicly since the 25th anniversary.

Melody and Kim always listen to "Mom's voice." After 40 years, believe it or not, I think I hear her too. My single biggest regret in life is that Jennifer never met Nudy and Bill. She would have loved them, and they would have loved her.

KIM ◆ There are so many things that come to mind as I reflect upon the journey of this book and the paths I took as a result of the crash of Flight 191. For me, of course, it's hard not to think about how decisions we make in life impact not only our own world but sometimes others' as well. I listened to my gut in the winter of 1979, and my action to call off a wedding ultimately resulted in my parents boarding American Airlines Flight 191. I have to believe that all the decisions leading up to that moment were part of God's plan. They could have booked other flights, picked a different destination, but they didn't.

I eventually turned to professional counseling, at times six days a week, with Dr. Neal J. Gordon to begin to heal and slowly put the pieces of my shattered life back together. I listened to my inner voice to get the help I needed to work through the guilt, pain, and trauma of the crash. With lots of encouragement and support, I began to heal, hear my own heartbeat again, and wanted to be a participant in the world. Listening to that inner voice has served me well for the past 42 years, both professionally and personally. Professionally, it led me to apply to Decatur Classical School. That action had a very positive and surprising effect when those incredible 6th graders found out about Flight 191.

My advice to my family, and anyone really, is to take nothing and no one for granted. Do your best to cherish every moment and every "Red Letter Day" of your own or a loved one's life. I read somewhere that you will never know the value of a moment until it becomes a memory. I think my tradition of always trying to write a toast commemorating a milestone or Red Letter Day in our family is my way of capturing those moments in writing for the person being honored, so they can reread it someday and replay the moment. Every year, the writing and reading of a Christmas reflection for our entire family is my way of validating how blessed we are and the importance of sharing those valuable memories. That yearly reflection celebrates our family today and, hopefully, our children (and their children) will someday understand how much we valued our parents and all those whose traditions we share and carry on. In writing this book, and all the Red Letter Day reflections in between, I hope they understand that every day with those we love is a gift, and tomorrow is not guaranteed.

The biggest story I've ever written is this one, along with Melody and Jim. The best part of reliving, writing, and reflecting on these past 42 years was doing it with both of them every Thursday for four years around my dining room table. Did we miss a few Thursdays? We sure did, but not many. We kept our commitment to writing our story and enjoyed a coffeecake, lunch, laugh, and of course, tears. Oh, how Mom and Dad would have loved these meetings! I'm sure they do!

MELODY • The biggest challenge for us was deciding what format to present what we had written, scanned, and copied to our family. Throughout the writing of this book, for 200 plus Thursdays, Kim would go to Staples to copy what we had written to edit together at our next book club meeting. As we neared finishing the book, we discussed how we wanted this final family book to look. At one time, we had thought about Staples putting it in print in a binder for our family, so they would have the facts of our Flight 191 journey.

However, at the 40th-anniversary memorial, I ran into Bev Ottaviano, who was a former coworker of mine at the Arlington Heights Historical Museum. She asked me how the book was coming along, and I told her we were getting to the end and unsure how to proceed. Being a writer and belonging to a writer's group, she told me to call her as she may have some thoughts on whom we should contact. So, during the pandemic, we met with Bev, who gave us Chris O'Brien's name from Long Overdue Books. Kim contacted Chris, and I believe she sent him some of our chapters, and he said he would be in touch. Not long after, we met with Chris. At that meeting, he told us, along with making a book for our family, he thought this could be a story the public would be interested in reading as it had historical significance, especially in Chicago.

KIM ✦ When we met for the first Book Club in September of 2017, little did we think that we would end up meeting, writing, and editing for 200 Thursdays. Those meetings resulted in a book to present to our family beyond our wildest dreams! We were so proud of finishing this historical book for our family, thanks to Chris O'Brien and Long Overdue Books'

Creative Director/book-design-extraordinaire, Annie Leue, plus the rest of their team! The unveiling of our book ended up being a big Red Letter Day for our family.

MELODY ◆ As anyone with a big extended family knows, setting dates for everyone to get together and celebrate is a job in itself. The larger the family, the older the grandkids, the more difficult. However, everyone knew we had finished our book and wanted to see the finished product.

Bob was turning 75 in September, and since that was a Red Letter day unto itself, we decided to make it a "Double Red" with the book distribution too!

Before receiving the book, Kim, Jim, and I had decided what would go into the Long Overdue boxes along with our book. Our plan: hankies for all the women/girls in the family, and a key chain replicating a bow tie for all of the guys. We'd have bookmarks noting our Red Letter Days, along with a letter from the three of us. The letter from the three of us explained about our book writing experience and why we wanted them to know how our journey with Flight 191 altered our lives and, therefore, impacted our family's direction and intent. We also included a framed picture of Mom and Dad.

Kim and I prepared my house for this celebration as we have done many times before for various holiday and family celebrations. Decor was a mix of 75th birthday colors of black, silver, and red being a major color depicting this special Red Letter Day!

We had some food out but told everyone when they came in to grab a drink but no food, as we didn't want greasy hands while unveiling, distributing, and handling the nice hardcover books! "Not eating" had never been a request before in my house.

Kim, Jim, and I were situated at the front of the room on stools where we had a large poster of Mom and Dad, the same photo from the book cover. We had a large low table with the eight book boxes under a large red covering. Every family unit would receive a book, and depending on the makeup of their family, received a particular number of hankies, keychains, and bookmarks.

Family Grand Reveal, 2021 (above and right)

I started the event with a toast to Bob on his 75th birthday:

"Today is a big Red Letter Day for the Borchers-Jockl-Smith Family. First, it's Bob's 75th birthday. I met you, Bob, when you were 21 years old, and in a blink of an eye — or maybe two or three — it's 54 years later! Let's raise our glasses. To Bob! Husband. Dad. Grandpa. Brother. Brother-in-law. And Uncle. Wishing you a wonderful birthday today and a happy and healthy 76th year (as Grandma Ryan would say). Cheers!!!"

Before we unveiled and distributed copies to each family, we shared some thoughts about writing this book together.

KIM ◆ I looked out at our big, wonderful family and began a toast.

"Recently, we read quotes from David Kessler who has written books about grief and his recent book 'Finding Meaning: The Sixth Stage of Grief' touched us and how we feel. He says 'Loss is what happens in life. Meaning is what we make happen after loss.' Focusing on meaning rather than the horrible aspect of Mom and Dad's deaths has enabled us to move forward. In this book, all three of us offered our perspectives of life after our parents' deaths. Part of our hearts will forever mourn our parents' deaths, but that hasn't stopped us from building wonderful lives and beautiful families. We wanted you all to have our story.

You've all heard about Flight 191 so many times in your lives that I hope this book gives you an insight into not only the facts of how our parents — your grandparents and great-grandparents — lost their lives, but how their kids, aka the three of us, survived the events of May 25th, 1979, and all that followed. It's a great story that I hope reminds all of you of the importance of family, Red Letter Days, and being there for each other.

At the time of the crash, the three of us were all in very different places, as you will read. The common denominator was Mom and Dad, our family, and our traditions/Red Letter Days. The love of that common denominator survived the crash and has guided and inspired us in so many ways. I hope our love does the same for all of you. I hope you all have an opportunity to hang with your siblings when your hair turns grey. We saw each other every week for the last four years and we hope you all will have activities together that you'll enjoy as much as we have enjoyed our Book Club.

My overarching advice is this: listen to those inner voices. We acted on recurring thoughts to do something so Flight 191 and our parents would never be forgotten. Maybe many others had the same thoughts but chose not to act, as we did. Since 2003, this journey achieved much more than we ever set out to do or imagined."

After the toast, I began by requesting a "drum roll, please!" from all in attendance. The three of us then removed the covering over the long low table. Everyone cheered. We distributed the boxes to families one at a time and shared how they're connected to our story:

"There are five people in this room who knew Nudy and Bill," I said to kick off the book reveal. "The three of us, Bob, and Chris. Bob, we present the first book to you and Melody, the matriarch!"

JIM ◆ "Christopher. Nudy and Bill adored you. Your christening was one of the last photos taken of them. And here you are with your beautiful family — Kelly, Camy, Elle, and Kinsley — 42 years later."

MELODY ◆ "Next book box goes to the Senior Jockls. Peter, we hope you enjoy reading the book, as for two years of this project you weren't home or around and when you retired, you graciously would leave or busy yourself so we could write, discuss, and then return home in time to join us for lunch!"

KIM ◆ "Jennifer, please accept the Borchers Book Box knowing that your magical Maui wedding to our brother 25 years after the crash is another big turning point for all of us. That's when we finished Nudy and Bill's flight to Hawaii!"

JIM ◆ "Jordan, early on in our story you arrive on the scene and brought new life to our family at a time we needed a shot of joy and happiness. Here's to you and your beautiful family — Taleah, Conner, and Maverick!"

MELODY ◆ "Matthew, you arrived nine years after we lost Mom and Dad. It seemed much longer than that as we had been through a lot by the time you arrived! Here's to you and Sheri and being part of our story."

I paused and picked up the final book box.

"And Jimmy, your arrival 14 years after the crash, brought another dimension to our family gatherings and more joy. Here's to you and Maya and being part of our story!"

KIM ◆ The books were distributed. Our incredible family started to flip through the pages and snapped photos with their copies and photos with us. There were hugs all around. And now we could dig into the food. Let the party begin!

Especially these last four years, the three of us knew we needed to write a book to document our journey so that our families will understand their history in regard to Flight 191 and how it influenced our lives and theirs. Having them all together, sharing a permanent document of our story, wow! What a grand Red Letter Day it was!

I'd say we safely landed!

RESTAURANTS & SPOTS: NUDY *and* BILL LOVED *to* FREQUENT

The Bergoff Restaurant
Blackhawk Restaurant
Black Angus
Brown Bear Restaurant
Buffalo Ice Cream Parlor
Burts Deli
Chez Paul
Como Inn
Continental Plaza Hotel, The
Consort for Brunch
Deasy's
Dohl's Morton House
Elks Club BPOE 1666/Cork Room
Elliott's Pine Log
Erie Café`
Fluky's
Fondue Stube
Grassfield's
Hackney's on Harms
Half Shell
How Lee
Italian Village
The Ivanhoe
Jerry's Deli

Jimmy Wong's
Johnny Lattner's
Kenilworth Inn
Laurie's Ice Cream Parlor
Laurie's Pizzeria
Martini's
Mecca Supper Club
Meson Del Lago
Miller Steak House
Millionaire's Club
Moody's Pub
Morton House
Myron & Phil's
Oddo's Pizzeria
Pickle Barrel
Richard's Drive-In
Schulien's
Schwaben Stube
Sieben's Brewery
Snuggery
The Office
Twin Anchors
Welcome Inn
Zum Deusch En Eck

Circa late 1950s

Circa late 1960s

AMERICAN AIRLINES FLIGHT 191 FRIENDS *and* FAMILY

KIM • The ongoing saga, for me, is the closed Facebook group I created called, "American Airlines Flight 191 Friends and Family." To the best of my knowledge, this is one of the only places people can connect with others connected to the crash of American Airlines Flight 191.

Twelve years later and now with over 400 members, it has served as a spot to share, remember, and exchange information about Flight 191.

It's the place where people share their stories of how the crash affected them after keeping it to themselves for 30-40 years. It's the place people speak of their guilt of not getting on the plane with their friends. It's the place people leave quotes and thoughts that have certainly stuck with me as I know they have with others as well. Quotes like:

"Our family needs to be able to connect with others from that day."

"There are no words to express the loss, the change, the way a family becomes different. I know you all understand."

"I am reminded I am not alone in dealing with this tragedy."

And one of my very favorite posted quotes: "If we live in the hearts we leave behind, we do not die." (Credit Thomas Campbell)

The group site has become a place for family and friends to post photos of their loved ones, and when the Memorial was dedicated, many proudly posted a picture of their loved one's brick to proudly acknowledge that they will never be forgotten. For many that have never made it to the wall because of distance, I have trekked out to the memorial, taken pictures of their loved ones' brick and sent it to them so they can see their loved one was not forgotten. I have sent over 40 pictures of bricks to those who request to see their loved ones' names. In addition to pictures of the brick that I email or message, I have mailed double that amount of programs, ribbons, and the story of how the memorial came to be to people who have found me, joined the group, but missed attending the 25th, the Dedication or most recently the 40th Anniversary. I have never said no to any request as I feel it is somehow my job–as long as I am able–to help people connect and find others connected to the flight.

This Facebook group contains hundreds of stories, emails, and passing moments with strangers, most I will never meet. I hope our brief exchange of words, program or picture sent, will help bring them peace and a connection that there are others who share with them the loss and heartache of May 25, 1979.

INTRODUCTION & MELODY'S SPEECH: 40TH ANNIVERSARY FLIGHT 191

5/25/2019

Good afternoon, I am Melody Smith. I am Kim Jockl. We are 2 of 3 children of Corrinne and Bill Borchers who died on Flight 191. Today I want to share with you the important people that initially helped us to commemorate the 25th anniversary at the airport which then ultimately leads us to this beautiful wall.

As the 24th anniversary neared my sister Kim & I knew it was now or never to reach out to family members and to share our stories and plan a memorial. While we were investigating the location of the crash site we were distressed to see construction material and the City of Chicago Water Reclamation signs. We thought we would now never get on the site. But as luck would have it, Terry O'Brien was the president of that committee and he and my sister had gone to elementary school together and more importantly he knew our parents. We asked him to check with the authorities at the airport to see if we could plan a 25th anniversary at the airport with hopes of getting on the site. In the meantime, Kim and I were going through old newspaper articles to acquire names to contact. We knew this would be difficult as our parents' names were never correctly listed in full. This also was just the start of e-mail and there was no Facebook, social media, etc. We first contacted American Airlines who said they could not give us the manifest legally until after the 25th anniversary. So, we then started writing letters to families of people mentioned in newspaper articles 24 years ago like the flight crew and local authors. We tried every avenue available to us at the time to locate people.

Terry O' Brien got back to us and introduced us to Leo Karral who is here with us today reading names and Jim Glowa, who were City of Chicago and O'Hare airport authorities. These 2 men supported the idea of a 25th memorial for flight 191 and they would arrange for everyone to get on to the site and so our journey to find more families who lost people on this flight continued.

The first person we made contact with was Michael Lux, son of the pilot Walter Lux. He in turn introduced us to Gary Schwartz, who lost his parents on this flight and Gary is also here today reading names. We then heard from Jan Dillard, the co-pilots wife who now was Jan Kransberger. This became the small group who were committed to a 25th memorial and finding family members along with the direction and help of Terry O'Brien, Leo Karral & Jim Glowa.

The 25th memorial had about 15 families represented. We had made contact with about 20-25 families. Not many, not enough but were thrilled with everyone we connected with.

When we started this journey, to recognize the 25th anniversary, it was about us and finding other people like us who lost someone on the flight but as time went on, we quickly learned that this flight impacted more than just family members. There were firemen, policemen, state troopers, first responders, second responders, residents of the surrounding trailer parks, and airport personnel and all of those groups were represented at the 25th and were appreciative of this memorial. At the time of this crash, workers were not to mourn publicly but rather to get back on the job without a break or help to heal from what they had experienced

At the 25th I expressed hope that American Airlines and possible O'Hare would assist us in the pursuit of a permanent memorial marker honoring 273 individuals connected with Flight 191. Thanks to Michael Lux through people he knew at American we for the first time at the 25th memorial actually had 273 names listed together.

At that point we knew we needed a memorial but where, what & how? And of course we still did not have the official manifest. But then something happened prior to the 30th anniversary and the rest is history.

KIM'S SPEECH: 40TH ANNIVERSARY FLIGHT 191
5/25/2019

Well, almost...there was a few more paths to cross and happenings before bringing us to today in Lake Park. The next thing that happened was Sue Kukielka hired me as the AP @ Decatur Classical School in 2005. As time went on I realized that being at Decatur was probably orchestrated from above by my Mom to have me cross paths and meet people that would be part of our Flight 191 Journey.

Fast forward to the spring of 2009: Melody and I are interviewed by Vince Gerasole from Channel 2 news regarding the upcoming 30th anniversary along a fence in the Oasis Mobil Park. The focus of the interview was the need for a Memorial. Little did I know or think that the interview would be a catalyst of things to come.

The following fall 2009, Mrs. Allegretti and Mrs. Sharping invited me to take part in a discussion with the 6th graders brainstorming ideas for their Constitutional Rights Foundation project for the year. Some students had seen the interview with Vince and I told the story of how there was still no Memorial 30 years later and why Memorials are so important.

The students decided to make a Flight 191 Memorial the focus of their project. The project went on to win National Awards and Recognition and as we all know, became a reality due to the support of US Representative Jan Schakowsky, Illinois State Senator Dan Kotowski, then Des Plaines Mayor Marty Moylan now State Representative Moylan and so many others!

On October 15, 2011 the beautiful Memorial was dedicated with the help of many but especially the Des Plaines Park District team and Gene Haring! Father Mike Zaniolo blessed the Memorial and sprinkled sod from the crash site as he will again today. We thank him for being part of our journey from the 23rd Anniversary to today and hopefully beyond.

Last May 25 while visiting the Memorial with Melody and Jim we crossed paths and met an Illinois State Trooper who was a first responder, a relative of a passenger and a CFD Aviation Fuel Safety Inspector, Ron Walerowicz paying his respects with a colleague. He asked if we were planning anything for the 40th, gave us his card and offered to help if we were. His inquiry spurred us to call Gene Haring and asked if he thought it would be possible to do something special for Flight 191's 40th Anniversary.

In true Des Plaines fashion he did not hesitate and answered YES! By the fall, planning was underway with Ron (yes he and the Chicago Fire Dept. played a big role in today's event) Gene, and his wonderful Des Plaines team: Brian Panek and Maureen Stern. Word cannot express our gratitude to them and the entire Des Plaines community for being part of this journey!!

We don't meet people by accident. They're meant to cross our path for a reason. The blessing of this journey for us is all the wonderful people we've met and stories shared since 2002...bringing us to today...this First Anniversary that ends in a Zero of which there is a place to gather, remember and never forget American Airlines Flight 191.

FLIGHT 191

FLIGHT CREW

Captain
Walter H. Lux

First Officer
James R. Dillard

Flight Engineer
Alfred F. Udovich

Flight Attendants
Robert E. Aeschbacher
Linda K. Bundens
Paula M. Burns
James T. DeHart
Carmen L. Fowler
Katherine A. Hiebert
Carol M. Ohm
Linda M. Prince
Michael Schassburger
Nancy T. Sullivan
Sally J. Titterington

(cont'd on next page)

PASSENGERS

Jeffrey N. Adams
James W. Adams
Richard Adams
Kathleen Adduci
Abdullah Al-Swailem
Ahamad Al-Swailem
Basil Al-Swailem
Mona Al-Swailem
Jessica A. Altman
Colleen Anderson
Gary Ang
Edward Armenta
Ruth C. Armstrong
Robert Artz
Sherry Atkinson
Ruth Baldini
George Barich
Robert E. Baum
Jeanette Bean
Charles Becker
Carroll D. Begley
Judith Bennett
Itzhak Bentov
Jeff J. Bett, Jr.
Stephen Blake
Paul A. Blovin, Sr.
Jim Bollinger
Bill Borchers
Corrinne Borchers
Edmund A. Bower
Reginald N. Braine
Oran Bridges

Allen E. Bryson
Eugene Bugaiski
Terrence G. Cady
Gerald Campbell
Bob Cannon
Carol Carlson
Dana L. Castronovo
Sheila C. Charisse
Charles Cheng
Ping Chun
Stephen Clark
Ira S. Cohen
Sara W. Collins
Dennis T. Connell
John L. Conner
Bruce D. Corrigan
Anthony A. Costello
David J. Coughlin
Francis L. Coulter, Jr.
Sedonna O. Crawford
James Crossley
Mario A. Crucioli
Elena Crucioli
Ed David
Marilyn H. Davis
Patricia C. Davis
Rhonda De Young
Joseph DeBerry
John DeVerrier
Gail S. Dhariwal
Gail S. DiCastro
Don Dick
Patrick S. Di Credico
Robert J. DiMiceli

Darlene DiPietro

Wilbur Dittmer

Lloyd Dixon

Jack Donahue

Donald Driscoll

James W. Dudley

Kathleen M. Dzwonkowski

Frederick Eaton

Amy Eisenburg

Rev. Edwards E. Elliott

Carl Entener

Terry Ernest

Marian E. Eshenaur

Dr. Roy Eshenaur

Susan Falcone

Carol Ferntheil

William Files

Larry M. Fink

Robert A. Fish

Sharon Fitzgerald

Richard J. Forstrom

Walter L. Frasier

Joan Fuselier

Kathleen Gallagher

Robert M. Gardner

Francis R. Gemme

Clem Glass

Craig Goetz

Mark S. Goldsmith

Joseph L. Gonzalez, Sr.

Lloyd E. Gray

Alan Green

Judy Green

Mike Green

Stephen Greene

F. Eugene Greenroyd

Kenneth Greger

Raymond L. Griego

William F. Guthrie

Victoria C. Haider

Paul Halopoff

Mattie Hammond

Jong Bin Han

Charles T. Harlin

Anna Harrison

George Hart

Nigel Hawkins

Dennis Hayes

Robert Hemphill

Samuel Henderson

Pete Herdman

Phillip Higginbotham

Edward Hill

Donald E. Hoover

Olin W. Hoskins

Elaine Howell

Eichi Ing

Stuart N. Janis

Ferdinand Jaworowski

Charles A. Johnstone

Hans J. Kahl

Richard B. Keely

Marc Kamhi

Howard F. Keeney

Jerri Koch

Thomas Koneski

Priscilla Kostohryz

Bert Krell

Dr. David Kuykendal

Rose Kuykendal

John Lakotas

Kenneth Lamb

E. Stephen Lang, Jr.

Susan Lang

Anthony LaVorgna

Margaret LaVorgna

Lorene K. Leiman

Richard E. Lent

Rev. Albert Leunens

Shu-Ren Lin

Henry C. Magner

Virginia K. Magner

Michelle Malacynski

Doreen Malek

Timothy J. Malone

Jacques Manning

Joel Markus

Laura Marquet

Jon D. May

Gordon McAtee

Marjorie L. McCorkle

William McGinnis

Marvin Milner, Jr.

Myron Miyagawa

Michael M. Mlsna III

Romeo Mon

John G. Moncrieff

Peter Moon

Debra A. Moruzi

Karl F. Muller

William C. Muller

Julia T. Nary

Willard R. Nary

Yvonne Nasch

Jeffery Nordhaus

Don J. Novelli

James O'Bannon

Margaret O'Rourke

Andrew Oliver

John R. Ondreck

Donald G. Optican

Julie L. Ozminkowski

John E. Pillivant

James Pint

William T. Pittenger

Marcia Ellen Platt

Eileen M. Plesa

Rossmoyne Pohlson

Constance Polley

Henry F. Regnery

Jack E. Reich

Allen Riddle

Alfred Rider

John Robison

Dean Rogers

Robert Rothfusz

Geertruida Rothfusz

Douglas Ruble

Jack Russell

Edwin Salisbury

Paul Schade

Zaida L. Schade

Marjorie Schade

Zaida Schade

Anne Schots

Wilhelmina Schots

Charles M. Schrader
Richard Schuster
Bernard Schwartz
Beatrice Schwartz
Vernon Sharpe
Ina P. Shatkin
Lloyd Shatkin
Wayland Sheffield
Mary Sheridan
Michael J. Silva
Larry Silva
Rodney S. Simmons
Michael S. Sirota
Michael Smith
Robert R. Spicuzza
Salvatore Spina
Margaret Stacks
Leonard Stogel
Jack Stone
John Stone
Eleanor I. Stromme
Chris Sutton
Colin Sutton
Stephen Sutton
Carolyn M. Sutton
William R. Swift
Michael A. Taylor
Kerry Tims
Paul Trammel
Paul R. Trautmann
Clark Turner
Margaret Tyne
Craig Valladares
Dr. Rene Valle

Margaret Valuch
Pieter Van Berkhoot
Dr. Robert W. Vaughan
Narda Vetor
Martha J. Vickery
Carl Vincent
Doyle Walker
Rebecca Washburn
Richard A. Watson
Judith Wax
Sheldon Wax
Dr. John B. Wear, Jr.
Richard J. White
Theodore Whyland
Ronald Willner
Dale Witthoft
Walter Yamashiro
Richard Zepnick
James M. Zielinski
Diane Ziemba
Jon J. Ziemba
Al Zvanut

VICTIMS ON THE GROUND

John Craig
Andrew D. Green

INJURED ON THE GROUND

Andrew Bellavia
Richard Maskeri

ACKNOWLEDGEMENTS

Thank you to all of our family, friends and strangers who crossed our path and played a role in helping us Land Safely and making sure American Airlines Flight 191 would never be forgotten. Thank you for being part of our journey!

MELODY, JIM & KIM

FAMILY

Peggy & Joe Anzelone
Jennifer Anzelone Borchers
Sue & Fred Collins
Kathy & Jim Hackett
Jimmy Jockl
Matt & Katie Jockl
Matthew & Sheri Jockl
Peter Jockl
Patty Ryan
Maya Salazar

Bob Smith
Bob & Marge Smith
Chris & Kelly Smith
Camy Smith
Elle Smith
Kinsley Smith
Jordan & Taleah Smith
Conner Smith
Maverick Smith

FRIENDS

Mary Frisby Bannon
Melissa Beckwith
Joe Boisso, CPD
Kathy Britt
Carol Contos
Kim Crawford Cook
Sharon Davis
John Gantz
Cathy Ciucci
Geryl & Bill Cerney
Mary & Peter Connolly
Cooney Funeral Home
Mary DuShane
Terry & Donna Gaertner
Bert Geldermann
Alison & Neal Gordon
Linda & Bob Hageman
Ron Halvorson
Fran Harwas
St. Hilary Church Community
St. Hilary Immaculate Heart of Mary
    Guild & Friends
Maureen Flynn Holman
Gail Hohenadel Hussey
Rev. Walter Huppenbauer

Tom Juliano
Nita & Dick Lamkey
Randall Leavy
Robin Love
Ellen & Ray McDermott
Vera & Mike Murphy
Terrence O'Brien
Cathy O'Connell
Patrick J. O'Connor
Cindy Beaulieu Oliver
Bev Ottaviano
Colleen Palmer
Pyster Family
LuAnn Presslak
Steve & Pam Rice
Lorraine Richings
Jack Sackley
Eddie Spencer
Hope Bendoratis Smith
Mary Steidele Quinlan
Pat Sturch
Meg Sturch Schaefer
Bobbie Sullivan
Ellen Teinowitz-Taylor & Andy Taylor
Fred Venrick
Judy Belzer Weitzman

LONG OVERDUE BOOKS

Annie Cerovich
Annie Leue
Chris O'Brien

Michele Popadich
Lauren Silverman

AMERICAN AIRLINES FLIGHT 191 25TH & 40TH ANNIVERSARIES

Jim Barry, CFD
Gail Dunham
Annie Durkin
Officer Fortuna, CPD
Tee Galley
Ron Gembala, CFD
Jim Glowa
Bill Hart
John Jakubec, CFD
Leo M. Karrall
John Kenney
Bill Klan
Kandace Kramer, Oasis Mobile
	Home Park
Charles Kransberger
Jan Dillard Kransberger
Bryson Lang
Joy Lang Holmes
Michael Lux

Sarah Magana/Rosehill Cemetery
Ed "Mac" McCall
Jack Ozminkowski
Brian Panek, Des Plaines
John A. Roberson, Chicago
	Department of Aviation
Charles Roy, CFD
Tim Sampey, CFD
Gary Schwartz
Cathy Stenberg, Triton College
Maureen Stern, DesPlaines
Ron Walerowicz, CFD
Rev. Michael G. Zaniolo, STL
Joseph Zurad
Chicago Fire Department
Global Travel Safety
Natural Air Disaster Alliance
O'Hare International Airport

MEDIA

Adrienne Balow, WGN
Kori Finley, Chicago Tribune
Vince Gerasole, CBS
Mike Lowe, WGN
Sarah Shulte, ABC

Todd Wessell, Journal & Topics
Arlington Heights Daily Herald
Chicago SunTimes
Chicago Tribune
Des Plaines Herald

DECATUR CLASSICAL SCHOOL/MEMORIAL WALL PROJECT

Al Albert

Beth Allegretti, Teacher

Jessica Chetnik, CRFC

Dave Davis

Decatur Classical School Students, Staff & Parents

Thomas Demetrio

Gene & Lisa Haring, Des Plaines

John Hecker, Des Plaines

Ilinois State Senator Dan Kotowski & Staff

Susan J. Kukielka, Principal

Lieutenant Joseph Locallo

Don Miletic, Director of Des Plaines Park District

Mayor Marty Moylan, Illinois State Representative

Janie Morrison

David Orr, Cook County Clerk

Roland Paulnitsky

Margo Regalado, Decatur Classical

US Congresswoman Jan Schakowsky & Staff

Marianne Sharping, Teacher

Danny Wallenberg, CCC

Abbott Molecular Inc, Des Plaines

American Airlines

Center for Civic Education

Chicago Public Schools

City of DesPlaines

Constitutional Rights Foundation, Chicago

Des Plaines Park District/Lake Park

Nilco Landscape Solutions

Project Citizen

Radisson Chicago O'Hare

Color Guard, VFW Post 2992, Des Plaines

Class of 2009-2010

Sunny Balan • Mark Bator • Hannah Baylor • Alex Behle • TJ Botten
Juan Cuecha • Nicholas Damen • Emily Etzkorn • Brittni Foster
Adriana Gerena • Dylan Gilbert • Leah Gomez • Leah Hahm
Ayomikun Idowu • Jacqueline Jones • Wes Jones • Lina Kapp
Matthew Koo • Natalie Lampa • Simone Laszuk • Esther Lawal
Christian Luciano • Emily Mack • Courtney Madl • Thomas Malthouse
Jenny Matusova • Saniya Merchant • Takahana Miller • Mugi Napolitani
Larry Ngo • Derrica Nickson • Andrea Nunez • Daniel Ogele
Heather Pollack • Alexandra Pollock • Shannon Robinson
Pilarina Romero-Sanchez • Christopher Rupprecht • Safiya Sirota
Adelina Socite • Claudia Sova • Ryan Toepfer • Gino Townsend
Mohammed Vaid • Will Wanberg • Tiger Wang • Ryan Wangman
Violet Wells • Adam Wesolowski-Mantilla
Anja Zehfuss • Alexander Zhang

Oh! How Mom and Dad would have
loved this group! I'm sure they do!!

The authors